The Deceiver

Rev. Livio Fanzaga

The Deceiver

Our Daily Struggle with Satan

Translated by W. F. E. Mahoney, M.A., S.T.L.

SOPHIA INSTITUTE PRESS
Manchester, New Hampshire

The Deceiver is a translation of *Il Fasario: La lotta quotidiana contro Satana* (Milan: Sugarco Edizioni, 2000), previously published by Roman Catholic Books, Fort Collins, Colorado, in 2004.

Cover design by Joshua Facemyer, Impressus Art LLC (ImpressusArt.com).

Sophia Institute Press
Box 5284, Manchester, NH 03108
1-800-888-9344

www.SophiaInstitute.com

paperback ISBN 978-1-64413-604-1

ebook ISBN 978-1-64413-605-8

Library of Congress Control Number: 2021950966

First printing

Contents

Introduction

Why, at every time and in every place, are human events filled with wickedness and suffering?

Evil—of which death represents the summit, its highest expression—is not the work of God, who created everything. "Through the devil's envy death entered the world, and those who belong to his party experience it" (Wisd. 2:24).

This new book by Fr. Livio, which is connected to his previous books, is dedicated to the mystery of the devil, of whom through revelation we have only a partial but irrefutable knowledge. Fr. Livio continues the task of casting light on some of the truths that form an essential and fundamental aspect of the Christian message and that today are often left in the shadows by contemporary pastoral practices, seeming to have small following in the life of the faith of the people of God.

Of course, focusing a work on Satan involves the risk of a somewhat false perspective in which, by the overestimating of Satan's importance, the main point of Christian life can seem to be an anxious vigilance in battle against the enemy who assails us, rather than the contemplation of a Love that saves us by happily and humbly calling us to respond to it. It is a risk of which the author is well aware; but he confronts and overcomes it, showing the admirable coherence that unites the diverse aspects of the Christian Faith. The entire vision of the relationship between God and man is recalled, and the theme in question—with its disquieting aspects—is presented within a framework in which the victory of God over evil stands out: "The victory of Christ over Satan is the very heart of the Gospel," emphasizes Fr. Livio.

The sources on which the author bases his presentation of Satan's nature and works are the Scriptures (an impressive number of citations, unequivocal in their significance) and the Magisterium of the Church in its most recent formulation, the *Catechism of the Catholic Church*. The two biblical accounts, namely the temptation and fall of our first parents in the Old Testament and the victory of Christ in the desert in the New Testament, are examined in depth, because they signify the two great stages of the history of salvation: the victory of the demon over Adam, and the defeat of the demon by the New Adam, Jesus. These two moments are the paradigm of Satan's activity regarding man. His activity consists essentially in the falsification of reality, presenting evil to man under the form of a completely desirable good: thus, Satan is the deceiver.

The book dedicates many pages to the subtle ferocity of the tempter and to the diverse strategies, subtle and violent, to which Satan resorts to destroy the life of man by tearing him away from God. While this detailed description inspires a healthy fear, Fr. Livio nevertheless limits our wicked adversary's field of action with great clarity. If Satan is powerful, God is all-powerful; although it is true that Satan is shrewd and cruel, it also is true that no matter how many tribulations he can inflict upon us, he is unable to bend our will and force us to do evil without our consent. Thus, the present activity of Satan and man's freedom find room in the infinite love of God, who allows all His creatures the real possibility of choosing to be for or against Him.

Fr. Livio explains the need of a hard yet hopeful struggle, adding suggestions of great wisdom taken from the ascetic teachings of the Church, in particular from the patrimony of virtues of the saints—the true champions of battle against the snares of the devil—and from his personal experience.

The book calls attention to a journey of awareness and responsibility in a determined countertrend to the culture and mentality of modern life.

Undoubtedly, to the neo-Enlightenment rationalism and neo-pagan hedonism of our day, the Christian doctrine concerning the devil seems a scandalous cultural backwardness. Many Christians who are influenced by the current mentality judge it to be out of fashion or embarrassing to give credence to this teaching of revelation and its practical implications.

But a faith mutilated in its contents is no longer faith. Reducing the Faith to personal likes and dislikes is equivalent to placing ourselves, instead of God, at the center of adoration.

Therefore, let us be led by the Spirit of Truth "to complete truth," where we meet Christ, the victor over sin, evil, and death.

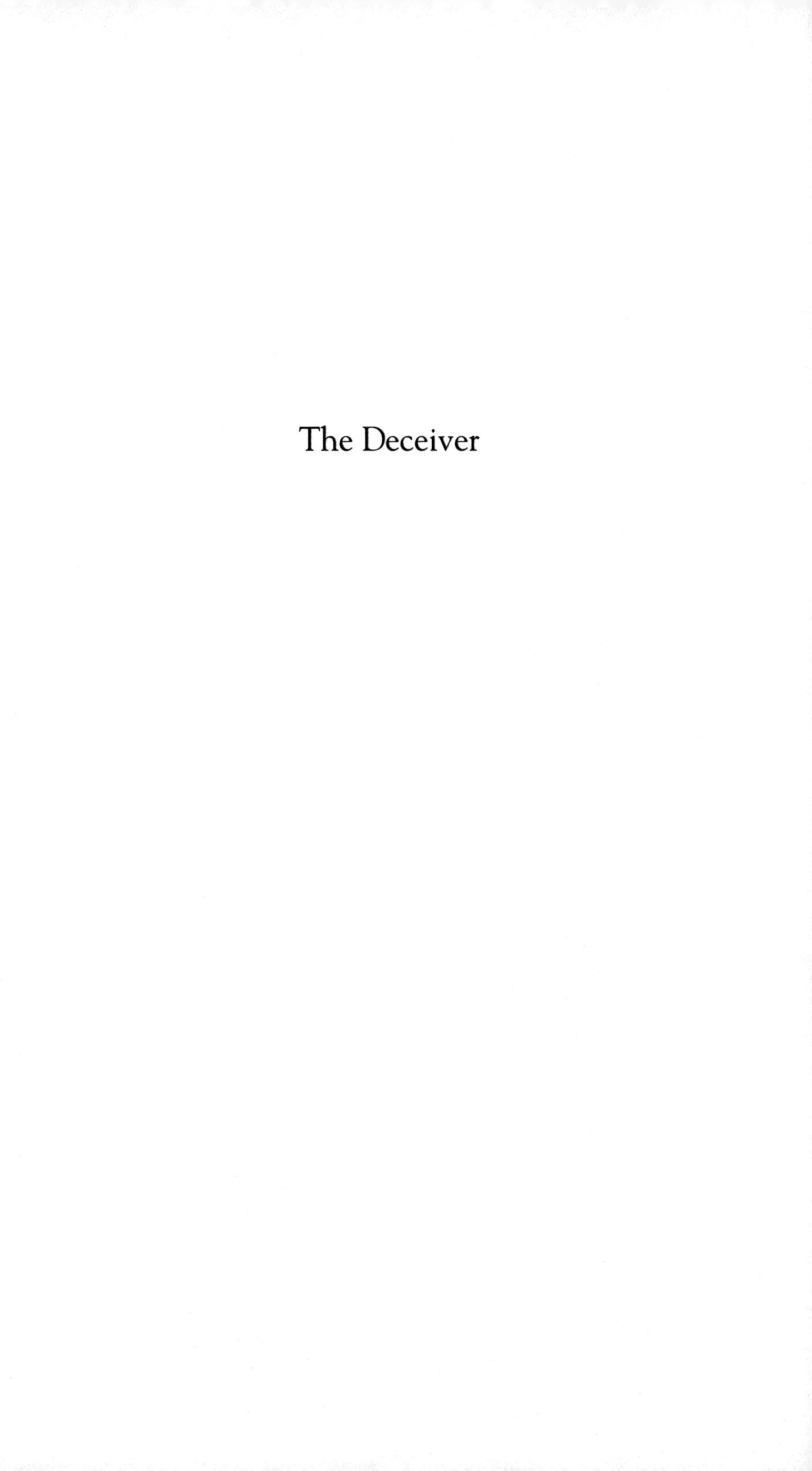

The Deceiver

1

Life Is a Struggle

The Reign of Heaven Is Won by Force

Christianity has been a militant religion since the beginning, but not in the sense in which Islam calls for a holy war against infidels, promising Paradise to those who fall in battle. Instead, the Christian warfare is of a moral and spiritual character, but it is in no way less demanding or important.

Reflect, dear friend, on the life of Jesus. It was exposed to dangers of every kind from the beginning. The power of carnal man felt itself menaced since His coming and searched with readiness and astuteness to eliminate Him. The three years of Jesus' public life saw Him pass through the daily snares of enemies and false friends, among whom some were disciples.

The prince of this world never stopped attacking Jesus. Satan confronted Him directly at the beginning of His mission and never ceased persecuting and trying to seduce Him, well hidden in unfaithful hearts. The Passion of Jesus is incomprehensible without the secret intervention and direction of Satan. The Incarnate Word and the rebel angel confronted each other in the most tremendous battle that has ever taken place in the world.

The pride of the creature and his hatred toward the Creator had their maximum expression in the days of the Passion. The ferocity of Satan, his wickedness, and his dark power are manifested exactly at the moment in which Christ's love for us arrives at its peak. The victory of Christ over Satan is that of love over hatred, truth over lies, and good over evil.

Christ is the great fighter. He did not struggle against the flesh, as every one of us who is weakened by Original Sin must do, but rather He had to fight against the world and against the demon. After the sin of Adam, humanity fell under the power of the evil one, who became the prince of darkness. Christ enters into the house of the powerful and binds him in order to take back that which is His (Matt. 12:29). With His death on the Cross, Christ obtains the definitive victory over the power of darkness (*Catechism of the Catholic Church* [CCC] 1708).

Do you think that this struggle is an exclusive characteristic of the life of Christ? He prophesied His persecutions and afflictions to His followers. All the apostles received the crown of martyrdom.[1] The same fate was suffered by many Christians throughout the course of the centuries, and those who have conducted an ordinary life in this world have also needed to fight the good battle to preserve the Faith and earn the Reign of God.

There is something false in the way many Christians of our time understand and live the Faith. Religion is seen as an exclusively consoling experience. I do not deny that one can find great consolation in an authentic Christian life, but that is the consequence of a persevering commitment on the good way. Many are ready to excuse moral disorder instead of fighting it. Heaven is promised to everyone, while silence veils the possibility of eternal damnation. Men appeal to Divine Mercy but continue in situations of sin.

[1] Except for the apostle John.

And how many regard Satan? Many are quiet about the enemy, as if he does not exist. The militant character of the Christian life is forgotten, but not for this do the enemies of man sleep. They are fiercer than ever. Against man, who is unarmed and unprepared for battle, their task has become easier than ever. The danger for souls is very grave.

Yet Jesus has warned us. With a mysterious expression, rich with power and meaning, He said: "The kingdom of heaven has suffered violence, and men of violence take it by force" (Matt. 11:12). No Christian, until Jesus returns to earth, will be able to consider himself on leave.

What Is at Stake in This Struggle?

Every war is engaged for certain goals which are more or less manifest. Men and nations do not hesitate to destroy each other for material goods, reasons of hegemony, dominion, or power. At the political and social level, as at the individual plane, which is more restricted but closer to our experience, we are ready to undergo the greatest possible efforts to defend our life or to improve it. How many risks and sacrifices are undertaken to obtain food, home, or work! The struggle of man for his survival is before your eyes every day and is often no less ferocious and ruthless than that which takes place in the animal world.

At a higher level, invisible but very real, we fight a much greater battle that involves Heaven and Earth. In this fight, the matter at stake is not something outside of you but you yourself. In this struggle, we can see that man is the most sought-after being that exists. Pick up the Bible and you will realize it. Even in the terrestrial paradise, man is snared by an astute and wicked enemy who wants to abduct man from God and subject man to his ruthless dominion. The final pages of Scripture demonstrate the final outcome of this interminable war, which sees the triumph of Christ and His enemies' descent into the lake of fire and sulfur.

At the center of this terrible contest between God and Satan, there are men. The history of humanity, from the Garden of Eden to the Heavenly Jerusalem, is the course of this great battle. After the catastrophe at the beginning of man's history, which conceded to Satan a certain power over humanity, came the moment of the victory of Christ and the redemption of man. We, dear friend, already enjoy some benefits from this triumph, but the dragon is only injured, and his ability to seduce and devour is still very strong.

It must be very clear that we are the prize of this competition. This is why we cannot remain indifferent or as spectators. The eternal destiny of every man depends on the outcome of this struggle. All the battles of life can be lost without irreparable consequences, provided one wins the most important battle, the unique one which is absolutely necessary to win: that which involves the eternal salvation of one's own soul.

Perhaps you are wondering why man is ever at the center of a war so severe that it covers the entire history of humanity, from its beginning to its conclusion. The key to interpretation is found in the first pages of Genesis, in which it is written that God created man in His own image and likeness, instilling in Adam, drawn from the earth, His divine breath. There is something divine in man; it is his soul. You, who are accustomed to considering material things as precious, perhaps do not fully grasp the infinite value of the soul. It is not, however, lost on the demon, who is pure spirit and who is in a position to evaluate the abyss which separates the spiritual soul from material creation.

What is the soul? It is not something you have, but rather it is you in the profundity of your "self"—able to comprehend, choose, decide, and love. Our soul is not God, but it is somewhat divine because it enables man to set himself in front of God as a person in front of another person, with the possibility of knowing, hearing, and receiving Him, but also with the possibility of refusing Him.

Thanks to his spiritual and immortal soul, man is before God in a free and conscious way. He can recognize God and accept Him as his Creator, Lord, Father, and Friend, but he can also reject His love. The soul is the most precious thing in creation. Furthermore, so great is the dignity of man that God was able to make Himself human. Such is the value of a soul, that even just for one soul, as some mystics affirm, Christ would have suffered His Passion and Cross. On the other hand, Jesus Himself is very clear and utters words that every Christian should write in characters of fire on his heart: "For what will it profit a man, if he gains the whole world and forfeits his life? Or what shall a man give in return for his life?" (Matt. 16:26).

Nothing in the universe is more important than a soul, and nothing is dearer to God than man. God loves man as a son and has prepared for man the greatest things His omnipotence could allow. Is it, in fact, possible for there to be a greater gift than the participation of man in the divine nature?

Satan is jealous of all this. He, who wanted to be like God, challenges Him, competing with Him for every soul, searching to seduce the soul in every way to make it his, to become its lord in his reign of death. Every soul torn away from Christ is a triumph for Satan. But he cannot seize your soul without your consent. Neither can God. This struggle between Heaven and Earth, which involves our eternal destiny, is ultimately decided by our free will.

The Enemies

Every war has its enemies. Even a spiritual war has its enemies. It would be a grave error to ignore or underestimate them. It is essential to be familiar with the enemies of our eternal beatitude so that we may avoid their snares and be able to face them with the appropriate weapons. The spiritual tradition unanimously points out three things to which we should never lower our guard. Those enemies are our flesh, the world, and the devil.

With regard to this, I declare without hesitation that the most insidious enemy of man is not the devil. After the Redemption, he is like a bound dog, which can harm only those who carelessly or willingly approach him. The most dangerous enemy of man is man himself. Our first parents, who were in a state of grace, with conscience and freedom, were the cause of their own fall, in spite of the undeniable ability of the tempter.

Our existential situation is much more vulnerable to the snares of evil than theirs was. In fact, even after Baptism, there is an inclination in man toward moral disorder because of his injured nature through Original Sin. The apostle John made especially clear the three types of concupiscence which stir in us: that of the flesh, of the eyes, and the pride of life (1 John 2:16).

The first enemy of man is his partially corrupted nature (CCC 405). We must be very vigilant regarding the infinite shrewdness of our flesh, always ready to deceive itself and us simply to be satisfied. When concupiscence, hiding in the deep darkness of our being, wants to obtain something, is it not always ready to present us with excellent reasons simply to achieve its objectives?

The undisciplined flesh is the most devious enemy of our eternal salvation. In its extraordinary capacity for arguing in a deceptive way, it will convince you that human nature, placed under the drive of concupiscence, will always fall into sin. It will make you feel so strongly its fallacious demands that in the end you will give up and acknowledge that the good is impossible. Certainly, it is impossible without grace, but it is possible to those who trust in God's assistance and are committed day after day to the spiritual combat.

There is another enemy that should not be underestimated. It is an enemy which is not in us but rather is around us and seizes us in such a smothering way that we cannot breathe. It is the world, in which we are planted like trees in a field. The world in itself is not evil, but sin has polluted it and permeated its social, economic, and political structures. The dominant culture, particularly the way of thinking and living promoted in the mass media, conditions our thoughts and our actions, molding a mentality in us which is often far from the wisdom of the Gospel.

You yourself realize how much influence can be exercised by a political leader or a television show. We often hear without realizing it, but afterward, we find ourselves thinking and speaking in exactly the same way. Even individuals, close friends, or fellow workers can influence our way of thinking and behaving, more often than we would be willing to admit.

So, dear friend, hidden behind the wickedness of the flesh and the false lights of the worldly fair of vanities, the untiring and ferocious adversary of God and enemy of man works. Satan is not a visible enemy like the flesh and the world, but he is very real. His shrewdness consists in hiding himself. In this way, he achieves the greatest success. Your task is to discover him in the innumerable situations of life, where he hides to set traps for you.

It would be misleading to attribute to Satan a power he does not possess. There is no doubt, however, that "by our first parents' sin, the devil has acquired a certain domination over man, even though man remains free" (CCC 407). He blows on the fire of your weak flesh and acts through the seductions of the world to snare you and take possession of your soul.

Do not fool yourself. If you travel the way of sin, it is Satan who keeps you on a leash. If you do not free yourself in time, you will belong to him for all of eternity.

The Final Goal

Spiritual warfare lasts until the final moment of life. The call of Jesus to be "vigilant" and "prayerful" concerns everyone, even the saints. Only those who persevere until the end will be saved (Matt. 10:22). It is not very useful for you to have won the initial battles if in the end you become lukewarm and then surrender. Paul reproached the foolish Galatians because, having begun with the Spirit, they ended as slaves of the flesh. Does not Jesus say, with one of His typically striking expressions, that "many are called, but few are chosen" (Matt. 22:14)?

It is incredible that man is disposed to fight the most dangerous battles and to undertake the greatest efforts simply to obtain a small piece of land, which nevertheless he will soon have to leave, while he does not care at all about the only war he needs to fight and the only battle he needs to win at any cost. Satan succeeds in deceiving man and brings him to the edge of the grave with the illusion that death is still far away, or that with death everything ends. What is there to say about the ones who die without faith, without prayer, without penance, and without hope?

A believer should not delude himself. At the end of life, at the moment in which spiritual warfare ceases, in the solemn moment of the last agony, every soul has already decided its eternal destiny. Either it will enter with God the Kingdom of Light, or it will go with the "cursed" into the kingdom of darkness. "Each man receives his eternal retribution in his immortal soul at the very moment of his death, in a particular judgment that refers his life to Christ: either entrance into the blessedness of heaven—through a purification or immediately—or immediate and everlasting damnation" (CCC 1022). If this is the final goal of life, do you not think that one should begin well in advance on the way which leads to salvation?

2

The Prince of Darkness

Satan Hides Himself

Unlike man, Satan does not love the stage. He does not avoid it for the sake of humility, because his great pride would never allow him to operate on that basis. He does it for usefulness, because hiding himself is useful to his purpose, that of enticing souls in order to capture them. Have you ever seen hunters showing themselves openly in front of their game? If they were to do this, their hunting bags would remain empty. They set themselves in hidden places and patiently wait for the unaware prey to draw closer. When they are certain that their prey cannot escape, they come out from hiding and deal their blow.

Satan is a hunter of souls and hides himself from professional cleverness. The ideal environment in which he can move around as much as he likes is that in which his existence is ignored or even denied. Do not think that he is offended if you neglect him. To the contrary, as Baudelaire accurately observed, Satan tries to convince the world that he does not exist. It does not bother him if he is underestimated. Being considered a "poor devil" does not put him in a bad mood. The essential thing for him is that the prey will fall into his traps, and then he does with them what he wants.

The Deceiver

The evil one finds himself particularly at ease in today's world. In a cultural climate which excludes the supernatural, he acts without being noticed. In a context of life in which God and His moral law are denied, Satan moves like a fish in water. Souls without light and deprived of the weapons of the holy battle are doomed. Seducing them with material goods and then chaining them up with sin is the simplest of enterprises for him. Who would not take by storm an army which has disposed of its weapons and has become lazy in idleness, in the deceptive conviction that the enemy is far away or does not even exist? The world has never been in danger as it is today, because the enemy of man is able to act undisturbed, where and how he wants, with no one to give a warning about his presence.

Scripture calls Satan the "ancient serpent" (Rev. 12:9). We do not know with certainty why the book of Genesis chose this image to represent the tempter. His discreet and silent tactic is nevertheless well represented by the movements of a serpent, which hides and camouflages itself, slipping into the smallest cracks. He does not need large passageways to penetrate the fortress of your heart. He does not care for assaults which are announced by the sound of a trumpet. He studies you in silence, without your being aware. His acute eye also sees the smallest holes to pass through. He waits for you to sleep, and then he slowly creeps in. When you are finally aware of his presence, it is already too late to escape from his venomous bite.

The reign of the evil one is presented by the Word of God as the reign of darkness. Satan loves darkness because he is able to hide himself in it. His ability consists in turning off the true lights which God has turned on in the world—the light of truth, the light of conscience, and the light of sanctity. As long as such lights are turned on and their flames burn brightly and vigorously, it is easier, even for foolish men, to notice Satan's traps. But if Satan succeeds in turning the true lights off, one after the other, and the power of darkness encompasses all things, woe to souls, because the dark one will be able to attack them as much as he wishes, without their being able to defend themselves.

The followers of the evil one are like him. They are ambiguous and hide themselves under false looks. They love to act in a hidden way, without your being aware. They hide well their thoughts, their feelings, and their works. Slowly they creep into your life without being noticed. You remain perplexed and wonder more often who they are. Remember, dear friend, that people who belong to God are always limpid and clear in their thoughts, in their words, and in their works. They act in truth and in light, while the sons of the evil one move about in darkness, faint light, and ambiguity. When you least expect it, you feel the sharp pain of their venomous bite.

Satan Eludes Human Knowledge

It is justifiably surprising if there are believers who deny the existence of Satan. Some theologians, dominated by a desire for novelties, have tried to explain to us that the devil is just a symbol of evil. Such explanations are pathetically inadequate if one looks at the numerous biblical texts that speak of the evil one and of his reign of death. I am less surprised when a nonbeliever or someone who is distant from God denies the existence of the devil.

The devil, save in some exceptional cases permitted by God, does not show himself openly, and his presence is not verifiable experimentally. He escapes human observation, and without the light of faith, you are not able to see into the profound darkness in which he is hidden. Therefore, we should not be astonished if the world does not know him, or denies his existence, or has a false conception of him. In a certain sense, though, this ignorance is astonishing because the devil manifests his great power as the prince of this world; but despite this power, men can discover and defeat him after the Redemption.

An apparently strange phenomenon takes place, one whose comprehension very much helps us to discover the strategy of Satan. After Original Sin, "the whole world is in the power of the evil one" (1 John 5:19). The Council of Trent does not hesitate to speak of a "slavery of man under the dominion of the devil" (Denziger 1510–1516). Nevertheless, men are not aware of it. The presence of the demonic in the different non-Christian religions is marked by many uncertainties, and those religions are very far from correctly grasping even the essential elements of the cruel face of the adversary of God and the enemy of man as he appears in the Bible.

All this has a very clear meaning. Satan loves to dominate individuals and society, holding them fastened between his claws but without even minimally revealing his presence. He successfully dominates people and the entire world without being noticed. The moment will come in which his followers will need to acknowledge him as prince of his reign of desolation, but for now he prefers to wait. Why? Because if men would recognize him now as he truly is, they would be seized by such horror that they would flee from him.

Let us reflect a moment on your life; perhaps all that we have said will be clearer to you. Has it happened to you to move away from God, taking the road of evil and sin? Without your having noticed it, Satan had seduced you with the false lights of the world. Influencing your passions, he had gradually taken control of your life. Little by little he entered into you, destroying all that the grace of God had made sprout and flower. Without your realizing it, you became ever more degraded, transforming yourself into the image of his darkness.

Yet at that moment you believed you were free, fulfilled, and even happy. It never crossed your mind, not even for an instant, that the evil one was fooling you, tossing you around like a leaf in the wind and preparing to destroy your life, bringing you down into the abyss of desperation. You laughed or perhaps sneered if someone spoke to you of Satan, but at that same moment, he was playing with you like a cat with a mouse.

Whoever is in the darkness does not see Satan and does not even suspect he exists. The world does not know its ruthless boss. While God has left His footprints in the world so that man, with the light of reason, can rise up to Him, Satan accurately erases every sign of his own presence. Even when he possesses a person's body, he seeks to remain quiet and unnoticed. Only the presence of the supernatural compels him to manifest himself.

Divine Revelation Exposes the Evil One

Knowledge of the reign of darkness comes to us through faith. Neither reason nor science could tell us anything of substance regarding this. You will justly wonder why a light that comes from on high is necessary in this field. The evil one plays a fundamental and central role in the history of salvation that has been revealed to us by the Word of God. We can say that if the presence of Satan is not recognized, the salvific action of God would remain incomprehensible to us. From what would God have saved us? From sin and from death, it is true, but haven't they both entered the world through "the devil's envy" (Wisd. 2:24)?

It is not astonishing that the presence of the adversary of God and the tempter of man is recalled by Sacred Scripture in the fundamental passages of the history of salvation. Beginning in the first pages of Genesis, a scene full of light and the splendor of creation, the evil one creeps in under the semblance of a serpent, incites a revolt against God, and succeeds in depriving man of his happiness. This initial catastrophe, in which man has lost God's friendship and eternal life, and which gives rise to an existence full of tribulation, took place under the clever and shrewd direction of the serpent.

We would know nothing about this if God had not revealed it. It is His Word which has revealed to us the presence of this powerful and ruthless enemy who is a constant menace to humanity. The development itself of human history is presented in Genesis as a struggle to liberate man from the tyranny of the serpent: "I will put enmity between you and the woman, and between your seed and her seed; he shall bruise your head, and you shall bruise his heel" (Gen. 3:15). This key to reading all of human history, given in the first book of the Bible, is resumed in solemn and magnificent terms by the last revealed book, Revelation, in which the great battle turns to the epilogue, with the definitive defeat of Satan and the final establishment of the Reign of God.

As you can see, Satan is the antagonist in the history of salvation. He is the adversary who is opposed to God, who can be defeated only by the strength of God. It is the light of revelation that makes known his presence, his malice, his methods, and his power. It is the Word of God that indicates to us the weapons with which we can fight Satan and that gives us the specific hope of final victory. Without the light of God, humanity would not know its enemy, who would be able to act undisturbed. Now that his presence and activity have been revealed to us, men who have faith can know him, fight him, and beat him.

The more intense the light of God, the more that Satan is forced to show himself. It is impressive to see in the Gospels how the entrance of the Son of God into the world shakes and agitates the power of darkness. At the very beginning of the public life of Jesus, after John the Baptist had just announced Him as the Lamb of God who takes away the sins of the world, behold, Satan comes out in the open. He confronts the New Adam, just as he had done with the first Adam in the earthly paradise. From now on, persecutions and seductions will alternate for three years, until the epilogue, when Satan enters Judas to bring to completion the great crime.

Jesus is the light of the world. His light shines in the darkness. He makes clear the hidden thoughts of men and their inspirer. His Word separates good from evil and good works from evil ones. Either one is with Him or is against Him. Either we serve God or we are against Him. Satan is forced to come out in the open. He is like that serpent whose hiding place has been found. His bite is always dangerous and fatal, but now you know that he is there and how he moves. The one who is strong in the Faith does not fall into the snares of the enemy.

If You Remain in the Light, You Will Discover Satan and His Snares

Today many, even among Christians, doubt the existence of Satan or have a mistaken conception of him. Some deny his existence, others underestimate his wickedness, others his power of evil, others even arrive at conjecture about his future conversion, in a kind of universal purification which will come at the end of the world. In our times of eclipse of faith and morality, there is no reason to be astounded that ideas of this kind catch on. When souls are in the darkness, or their faith is reduced to a smoking wick, they no longer see the evil one and his dark actions.

The Deceiver

If you read the Gospels and the other writings of the New Testament with attention, you will realize with what firmness, precision, and profundity the nature of the demon and his actions are described. This is also true for the lives of the saints. Perhaps you wonder why in the lives of the saints the evil one is always a hostile presence waiting to ensnare them. Sanctity is a light that illuminates the darkness, through which the evil one is identified and discovered.

This has great importance for the spiritual life of every Christian. If you live in tepidity or sin, you become an easy prey to an enemy you do not see, who entraps you without your being aware. But if you remain firmly in the light of faith and you are firmly committed to make your life always more pure, your eye will begin to see clearly the daily traps and the infinite shrewdness of the enemy, his inexhaustible resources, and the ferocity with which he avenges himself of all his defeats.

Of course, it would be a mistake to see the demon everywhere; but if your eyes are firmly set on the truth of God, you will have a timely awareness of Satan's seductions. You will discover his traps in the places where you have to be, you will resist with determination in the moments of the attack, and you will be able to use the weapons of light when he seeks to take you by surprise.

Many wonder with a certain apprehension how it is possible to avoid all the traps of such a shrewd enemy, so untiring and resourceful. It must not be forgotten that Satan can boast the capture of prey of great prestige, successfully destroying one apostle and dispersing like leaves in the wind all the others. [St. Louis de] Montfort notes with sadness that gigantic trees in sanctity are miserably broken, and eagles that soared in the heavens of the spirit are transformed into birds of the night.

The first defense against the evil one is the light of faith. He is the prince of darkness and of the one who has not persevered in the truth (John 8:44). If you are firmly rooted in the Faith, feeding it with humble prayer and the grace of the Holy Spirit, God will point out to you the traps of the evil one, even where your poor human eyes would never have never penetrated. God will reveal to you the most insignificant plots of daily life, where Satan hides himself with an unsurpassable ability. God will give you the discernment of persons, and He will ring an alarm bell in your heart in case of danger.

When the light advances, darkness inevitably retreats, and its secrets are revealed (1 Cor. 4:5). Be vigilant that your lamp does not go out and that your light is a true light (John 1:9).

3

The Origin of Evil

All of Creation Is Good

The origin of evil is one of the more recurring and anguish-filled questions of humanity in the course of its history. It is not an abstract problem, it is rather a clamor arising in the heart of suffering and injured man. "Why is there suffering, evil, and death?" Beneath these universal questions is the experience of men of all times, who realize that their life is crucified from the moment of birth until the moment of death. Coming into the world, man discovers himself a passing being, fragile and limited, and any attempt to radically change his existential condition, after the first illusions, ultimately results in a checkmate.

Human reason has wandered for a long time in uncertainty, and the first exhaustive answers have been found only by entering into the Faith and holding fast to the light of the Word of God. It is not merely a question of giving an explanation to the fragility of an endangered existence, as Buddha observed, "to sickness, old age, and death," but also and above all of seeking to understand the origin of that inclination toward moral evil that every man carries inside himself from the moment of his birth.

Some religions, in their groping in the darkness, have hypothesized the existence of a twofold divinity: a good one who has created everything that is good in the world, and an evil one who is the author of everything evil. This Manichean concept of reality has made evil something absolute, giving it an unlimited power and dimension. In this light, Satan, however he is conceived or called, becomes the competitor of the good God in a wrestling match between good and evil with an uncertain outcome.

The light of revelation, which shines in the first pages of the Bible, reassures us about the reality in which we find ourselves and to which we belong as creatures. First and foremost, we are reassured concerning divinity. There is only one God, who in His essence is goodness, beauty, truth, and love. There does not exist an evil god but a good God, in the fullest sense of this word. At the root of everything, there is no evil, only good; there is no darkness, only light; there is no pain, only happiness; there are no lies, only the truth.

Not only is God an ocean of goodness and beauty, but also everything which He has made from nothing with great power, wisdom, and love has the traits of goodness and beauty. The book of Genesis never tires of repeating that everything God has created is good, specifying, in the case of man, that he is "very good" because he is created "in the image and likeness" of God Himself. You will be wondering: If God is good, as is everything He created, what is the origin of evil, which is something every man experiences here on earth?

The Fall of the Angels

In the pages of Genesis, you will note that in the immaculate splendor of creation, where man occupies a central place through his natural dignity and through the gifts of grace he has received, there is a dark and unsettling presence. The earthly paradise represents the crowning of God the Creator's design. God places man in an existential situation of natural and supernatural happiness. In fact, beyond the sublime grace of the divine friendship which gives him the possibility of living in a close relationship with God, man possesses extraordinary gifts, such as wisdom, immortality, and integrity, which crown him with divine glory on an earth which still has the wholesomeness of creation before sin.

Yet evil is already present before the Fall of our first parents. In fact, beneath their disobedient choice, there is a seductive voice which opposes God (Gen. 3:1–5) and which, because of envy, causes them to fall into sin and death (Wisd. 2:24). There is ample evidence that it is an intelligent and malicious reality erected against God, putting in doubt His goodness and truthfulness. In the meantime, the evil one dangerously menaces man, seeking to deprive him of the divine friendship and of the gifts which he has received. "Scripture (John 8:44; Rev. 12:9) and the Church's Tradition see in this being a fallen angel, called 'Satan' or the 'devil'" (CCC 391). What is his origin? You will realize that in responding to this question, we are in a position to cast a beam of light on the mystery regarding the origin of evil.

In your Sunday profession of faith, you affirm that you believe in God the Creator of Heaven and earth, of all things visible and invisible. What are the invisible realities created by God? They are the angels. There is no doubt about their existence; they are presented as messengers of God in the entire span of the history of salvation as testified by Sacred Scripture. Angels are beings in the sphere of creation. This means that every one of them has been created directly by God out of nothing. They are pure spirits, endowed with intelligence, consciousness, free will, and without the limits or the potentialities of the body, which is something that is proper to man. They are more powerful and intelligent than men (St. Thomas Aquinas) and "surpassing in perfection all visible creatures, as the splendor of their glory bears witness" (CCC 330).

Created by God at the peak of perfection and thus given beauty, goodness, and splendor, some of the angels, by their own autonomous decision, have become evil. God did not create Satan as he is now, because God, being infinitely good, could not create an evil being. Satan has become as he is by his own choice, because he "has nothing to do with the truth," as Jesus affirmed (John 8:44). He has perverted himself. "The devil and other demons were created naturally good by God, but they transformed themselves into evil" (St. John Damascene).

When did this happen? St. John affirms that "the devil has sinned from the beginning" (1 John 3:8). Certainly this event happened before man was placed in the earthly paradise, because at that moment, Satan was already in action on the earth. The Word of God casts beams of light here and there on this original catastrophe of the angelic spirits, through which evil has entered the world. Peter the apostle affirms, "God did not spare the angels when they sinned, but cast them into hell and committed them to pits of nether gloom to be kept until the judgment" (2 Pet. 2:4).

Revelation presents a grandiose scene in which is placed the great battle between the good angels and the perverted ones. "Now war arose in heaven; Michael and his angels fighting against the dragon; and the dragon and his angels fought, but they were defeated and there was no longer any place for them in heaven. And the great dragon was thrown down, that ancient serpent, who is called the Devil and Satan, the deceiver of the whole world—he was thrown down to the earth, and his angels were thrown down with him" (Rev. 12:7–9).

What was the sin for which the "star" fell "from heaven to earth" (Rev. 9:1), receiving the keys to the pit of the abyss? There are many theological opinions concerning the sins of the angels, even appreciable ones, but if we examine the Bible with attention, there are sufficient clues for a basis of understanding. Regarding this, the words the tempter uses when he addresses our first parents are very eloquent, "You will be like God" (Gen. 3:5). What does this mean? St. Thomas Aquinas said that Satan desired to be like God and to participate in His beatitude not through a gift of grace but rather by taking it with his own natural power. Jealous of God, Satan wanted to obtain the splendor of divinity, not receiving it with submissive humility but stealing it with presumptuous pride. His sin was longing to have and possess more. Therefore, it was primarily a sin of pride by which the angel transformed himself into a demon.

We cannot know any more about the origin of evil. What is revealed to us, even if it does not satisfy all of our curiosity, is fundamental. Everything God has created is good. Evil originated with the decision of those creatures, angelic and human, who, being given free will, wanted to disobey God. Evil is a possibility of the free creature for as long as the time of his trial lasts. The trial for the angels was resolved in an instant; for men, it continues their entire lives.

Certainly we can reflect more deeply on the original perversion; but from revelation, the truth of the Faith emerges with indisputable clarity: that the angels were created good and that some of them have fallen: "this 'fall' consists in the free choice of these created spirits, who radically and irrevocably rejected God and his reign" (CCC 392).

The Irrevocable Character of the Choice

Some have thought that Satan can be converted at the end of the world when, as the apostle Paul affirms, God will "be all in all" (1 Cor. 15:28, NABRE). Even some people as far away in time as Origen and Papini have supposed this. Against this hypothesis is the teaching of Sacred Scripture and of the Magisterium of the Church regarding the eternity of Hell.[2] That "depart from me, you cursed, into the eternal fire prepared for the devil and his angels" (Matt. 25:41) solemnly pronounced by Jesus resonates with too much clarity to be hidden or merely tamed.

Others wonder why Satan and his angels were never forgiven after their fault while for man there was the Redemption, and such people ask themselves if they are not facing a possible defect in the mercy of God. The angels are like men in that before being admitted to the ineffable gift of the Beatific Vision of God, they must necessarily pass through a trial.

For the angel, given its spiritual nature, the *status viatoris*, that is, the time of the trial, lasted only an instant, in which the angel, a pure spirit, made an irrevocable and immutable decision. Having made this choice with perfect comprehension and absolute freedom, the time of the trial ended, and the angels remain ever adhering to the choice they have made. For this reason, St. Thomas Aquinas observed that the good angels, having adhered irremovably to the good, are confirmed in it, while the bad angels, having sinned, remain obstinate in evil.

For man, it is different. His sin is less grave than that of the angels because he is an incarnate spirit and his will adheres to one

[2] Regarding the eternity of Hell, like everything connected with the Last Things, see my book, *Sguardo Sull'Eternità* (Milan: Sugarco Edizioni, Milan 1993).

thing in an unstable manner, maintaining the faculty to detach himself from that thing in order to adhere to a contrary thing. You will note from your personal experience that you need to make many good choices to become stable in the good. In the same way, man does not become evil all at once but makes evil choices one after the other on the road to evil.

For this reason, the *status viae*, that is, the time of the trial with regard to man, is much longer and lasts for the entire duration of his pilgrimage on earth. He too, however, at the moment of death, will remain eternally stable in the choice he has matured during his life, that is, either in the humble and filial acceptance of God's love, or in its irrevocable refutation.

We live in a historical period in which irrevocable choices are feared. Such choices, however, are part of the divine economy. Jesus put before His hearers many times the decision of faith, by means of which one has salvation or eternal perdition. For the pure spirits, everything was resolved in a mere instant, while for us men, the decision emerges in the course of time, in the brief span of our lives. You need to come to a decision with God. He has given you free will and has confronted you with the supreme choice, by which you decide for all eternity.

For this reason, do not let the following teaching of the Church strike you as too severe: "It is the irrevocable character of their choice, and not a defect in the infinite divine mercy, that makes the angels' sin unforgivable. 'There is no repentance for the angels after their fall, just as there is no repentance for men after death'" (CCC 393).

"The Great Dragon ... Thrown Down to the Earth"

You will have realized that the origin of evil can in no way be attributed to God, who has made all of His creatures "good." It arises from the freedom, although imperfect, of both angels and men, which because of its limitations risks failure, as St. Thomas Aquinas observed. In order to impede evil, God should have avoided creating any free and intelligent creatures, but in this way, He would have also removed the possibility of doing good.

Free will is necessarily a two-edged sword. If you want to give a person the possibility of becoming your friend, you must necessarily leave him with the capability of saying no to you. Love is authentic if it comes from a free choice. To obtain our love, God exposes Himself to the risk of our senseless refusal. There is no doubt that God has risked very much in creating intelligent and free creatures in His image and likeness. It is a risk that parents know very well, a risk they share with God. Not all children are as we would like, and many make us shed tears.

Perhaps it is more difficult for you to understand why God, instead of immediately casting the dragon with his angels into the abyss, as will happen at the end of the world (Rev. 20:10), has left them freedom of action on this earth. You see Satan in action from the beginning (Gen. 3), in his homicidal activity (John 8:44), perfidious and untiring. Why does God allow Satan to act through all of human history? Why does He concede to Satan the ability to drag us into evil and allow him to hunt our souls ruthlessly? Why does He give him the opportunity to build a kingdom of death contrary to the Kingdom of God?

These are questions which are not easy to answer, because our ways are not God's ways and our thoughts are not God's thoughts (Isa. 55:8). Satan has sought from the beginning to oppose the plans of God the Creator. The proud and the reckless have launched the challenge. God has accepted it, realizing His design hidden from all eternity, "to unite all things" in Christ (Eph. 1:10). This project of infinite love will be infallibly carried out in spite of the opposition of Satan, who by his own choice will remain with all of his followers excluded from it, so that in the end, even he will give testimony to the glory, omnipotence, and justice of the Creator.

4

The Adversary of God

The Hatred of God

While God reveals Himself to man, Satan deftly hides himself behind people, things, and events. He is a liar and the father of lies (John 8:44); for that reason, his speech hides his true feelings, his real intentions, and his objectives. When he manifests himself, he assumes the external appearance of an "angel of light" (2 Cor. 11:14). If Satan succeeds in inducing man to sin and in silently taking possession of his life, it is because he is very dexterous at proposing evil under the appearance of good, enticing man with illusory happiness, successfully presenting himself as a benefactor.

It is strange, if you think about it, that the one whom Scripture presents as a roaring lion and an infuriated dragon is often described in common language as a "poor devil." The world knows so little about Satan that it has denied his existence or has reduced him to an innocuous character, like those ferocious beasts in the zoo, without claws and without teeth, who are stuffed with the snacks of children.

To know the evil one in the depths of his profundity, it is necessary to follow attentively his manifestations throughout the history of salvation. It is the light of God, particularly the light of

Christ, that reveals the true nature of this liar. In the same way, you will know him in the lives of the saints and even in your own existence, if you are seriously busy in the spiritual life. The false representation of the evil one that many Christians have constitutes a danger for their souls. Identifying him in his true nature is fundamental for success in defeating him in spiritual combat.

If I had to describe in a few words Satan in his essence, I would begin by saying first and foremost that he is the irreducible adversary of God and consequently the merciless enemy of man. If God is love, as St. John the Evangelist affirms, Satan, within the limits of his creaturely condition, can be defined as hatred. What is hatred? We know it through our life experiences. It is a destructive force which is born and grows in us and which, if it is not restrained, produces the most nefarious effects. Look around and evaluate for yourself what immense damage hatred produces in people, families, and society.

The first creature to have generated hatred in himself is the rebellious angel. It is hatred of God, born from the jealousy of not being God. Satan became like this when he did not accept that submissive humility toward the Creator who would have led him to a relationship of infinite love with God. The proud one does not tolerate that there is a God above him, he does not accept dependency, he refuses to serve. If he could eliminate God, he would do it. Not being able to exterminate God, not having the possibility of destroying Him, Satan fights God with all of his might, opposing God's plans and seeking to make His designs useless.

Satan knows that God is God and that he is just a creature. He is conscious of it, but he does not accept it. He would like to be in the place of the Creator. This not being possible, he emits from his being an inextinguishable hatred.

It is the same hatred he instills in the hearts of many men who proclaim themselves atheists, saying that they do not believe in God. In reality, they cannot bear that there is a God above them, a God on whom they depend and to whom they will have to render an account of their actions. They make themselves something absolute, final, and omnipotent. They say that God does not exist, but in reality, they hate Him, they fight Him, and they blaspheme Him. Satan is their prototype, and he communicates to them that implacable hatred he generates in the abyss of his perversion.

The Thirst for Adoration

The hatred of Satan for God and His works is so strongly demonstrated by Scripture and the spiritual tradition that it is not necessary to use many words to explain it. It seems more important to me to seek to understand the profound motivations of an adversary who would cause us to die of fright if we could know him even a little.

The genius of the author of Revelation has succeeded in giving us a suggestive representation of that irreducible hatred in the image of the enormous red dragon who sets himself in front of the woman about to give birth in order to devour her newly born baby (Rev. 12:4). Satan, who seeks to devour Christ and the Church, is not the biblical author's concession to mythical thinking but rather the true perception of that struggle without quarter that the rebellious angel has declared against God his Creator.

What is the reason for this hatred? There are many hypotheses about it, all of which converge in pointing out that pride is the source of the rebellion. Perhaps Satan refused to cooperate with God's plans that foretold the Incarnation and, in consequence, his submission to the Incarnate Word and to His Mother, as some spiritual authors suggest. It is difficult to be certain about this, but there is a passage in the Gospels that casts a beam of light on the origin of this satanic hatred. It is in the passage about the Temptation, during which, confronted with the light of Christ, Satan manifests his more recondite thoughts.

Having taken Jesus to a high mountain and shown Him all the kingdoms of the world with their respective glory, Satan says to Him, "All these I will give you, if you will fall down and worship me." But Jesus says to him, "Begone, Satan! for it is written, 'You shall worship the Lord your God, and him only shall you serve'" (Matt. 4:8–10). Here we can say well that Satan is exposed, as in no other part of Scripture. Here we have a complete exposure of the profound thirst and inextinguishable torment that dominate Satan. He wants to be adored. He does not accept being a mere creature and cannot bear that there is another, and not he himself, who is God. His torture consists in not being able to proclaim himself God, but nevertheless, he seeks to quench his thirst by tricking creatures and asking for their adoration.

This satanic hatred is not grounded in a jealousy of man but rather of God Himself. Satan is envious of God. Since this envy is murderous, he wants to annihilate Him. Not being able to do it, Satan challenges God, seeking to kidnap His creatures and opposing the magnificent design of Creation and Redemption with all of his might. In his reign of death, he demands adoration and absolute submission. Oh, how much it must torment him to realize that the power does not belong to him but to God, Christ, Mary, and the Church!

Do not think that the dragon holds all of this poison inside of himself. He abundantly injects it into the veins of men. How else would you explain the great rebellions against God that characterize some periods of history, particularly ours? Was not perhaps the project of wanting to build a world without God— a project that smolders in the stomach of humanity and in which man is lord and redeemer of himself—put into action by the ancient serpent? From where else would it come, this desire of men to excel, to be venerated and honored, to lord over and dominate others, as if making themselves little gods?

Every spiritual creature that possesses intelligence and will, be he an angel or man, is placed before a radical choice that imprints a precise direction in his being and in his acting. The choice is between God and your own self. Whoever chooses God, accepting the status of a dependent creature, enters into the light of grace and receives as a gift a participation in the divine nature. Whoever chooses his own self, deluding himself in thinking that he can eliminate God, enters into the darkness of self-exaltation and of spiritual death. Here we have the lie of Satan and of his followers who, being creatures, deny dependence and obedience, claiming an absolute freedom and demanding adoration.

The One Who Opposes the Plans of God

Satan is a Hebrew expression that means "the adversary." He is the enemy of God par excellence. The word *devil* comes from Greek and means "the one who divides," who puts himself crosswise and divides. These two words complement each other in making clear the evil one's activity. He hates God and seeks to impede and destroy with all of his power God's plans of salvation and merciful love toward man. Satan exploits until the very end the divine permission to work on earth to seduce souls, diverting them from the way of God and finally taking possession of them and making himself their sovereign.

The Deceiver

In the entire history of salvation, from the earthly paradise until the Second Coming of Christ, Satan is present and active. God's grand appointments find him always ready and never fatigued. It could be said that he never rests. His shrewdness consists in exploiting to the full extent the divine pedagogy respecting human liberty. Knowing well that man in his freedom searches for good and happiness, Satan leads man astray by presenting to him evil under the appearance of good. Wherever God works, Satan is present to impede the realization of God's merciful plans.

The opening of human history sees Satan's great victory. He succeeds with supreme ability in destroying the design of love that God had realized for man. What more could man have demanded from God, having received His intimate friendship and all the gifts of grace that caused man's experience on earth to be one of authentic happiness, in expectation of the Beatific Vision? Yet Satan succeeds in convincing man that God has not given him enough, because if He had, God would be jealous of man. Satan insinuates doubt into man's heart, arousing immoderate desires in him and pushing him to disobedience, and he gains his own objective—to ruin the project of the Creator.

When the New Adam stands out on the horizon, Satan immediately descends into the field personally, without hiding himself and very determined to launch a challenge. Where the sweet odor of sanctity expands, Satan hastens, because his kingdom is being menaced. The coming of the Son of God on earth is the much-feared moment. It is the hour in which the power of Hell is put into question. The demons know that they are not confronted by a mere prophet but by the One who has the power to evict them with a mere nod of His will. Yet Satan does not disarm himself and tries every possible avenue to impede the work of Redemption. The life of Jesus, especially the three years of His public ministry, was first subjected to the charm of seduction and then to the violence of persecution. His Passion would be incomprehensible apart from the reign of the prince of darkness.

After Christ ascended into Heaven, the Church became the number one enemy to fight. She is the prolongation of Christ, she is the pillar of truth and the fountain of sanctity. Men receive from her treasures of the Redemption. Satan realizes that fighting the Church allows him to maintain his dominion over the world. You can see how he operates from the very first hour of apostolic preaching. He seeks to seduce, to creep in, to create disorders, and to impede the diffusion of the Word of God. St. Paul, writing to the Thessalonians, confides to them that he had desired to visit them twice, but Satan impeded his going (1 Thess. 2:18).

The devil hates the Church with the same intensity that he hates God. How else could you explain the constant persecutions which have marked the way of the Church in the first two millennia of her history? Have you not observed how people who are under Satan's influence have a strong disliking for the Church and willingly speak against her, criticizing what she does or says? Churchmen are naive who hope to have the approval or admiration of a world still largely under the influence of the evil one.

The more the Church is of Christ, the more Satan hates it. The holier the Church is, the more Satan will accuse her, the more he will defame and attack her. The end of time will see the attempt of the evil one to eliminate the Church, with the greatest work of seduction and of persecution that has ever been (CCC 675). During this extreme assault, a last attempt to destroy the presence of the Church on earth, the army of evil will be suddenly swept away by the coming of the Divine Judge, who will decree Satan's definitive defeat, binding him forever in the lake of fire and sulfur (Rev. 20:10).

I would like you to understand that the untiring adversary of God is present not only at the great moments of salvation history but also in the little events of the daily lives of all who are in the service of God and who are committed to the road of sanctity. Where a work of God begins to take root and grow, there immediately the evil one draws close to impede the growth. Wherever Mary, the Mother of the Church, plants seeds of grace, Satan furtively approaches to steal them. In the hearts in whom the Holy Spirit spreads seed of sanctity, Satan immediately arrives to carry them away (Mark 4:15). With increasing faith and discernment, it will not be difficult for you to see the veiled and untiring work of the adversary, who attempts to impede your progress on the way to perfection.

The Alternative Kingdom

The adversary of God, who searches by every possible means to hamper the plans of love that God offers man, does not limit himself to destruction but intends to build something for himself. To affirm that Satan builds is using an improper expression, because the effort of building always implies something positive. Yet this word can be used because the evil one is not limited to destroying everything that is of God but searches in every way to realize a kingdom of his own, an alternative to that of Christ.

It is the kingdom of evil, of darkness, of slavery, of blasphemy, of hatred, and of desperation. Satan's untiring activity is geared toward the establishment of this kingdom, which will be his loot for all eternity. He believes that he can satisfy his hatred by showing God his prey, whom he has torn away from Him with their consent.

If Hell, on the one hand, is the place of divine justice, on the other hand it represents the eternal challenge with which the proud one defies God. The craving to construct a kingdom of his own, where he is the absolute boss in opposition to God, is the secret motivation which makes him untiring. His pride still blinds him, because even Hell can subsist only through a permissive divine mystery. Even the demons and the damned do not cease to be creatures who in their being are dependent on God. Be on guard, dear friend, not to let yourself be trapped in this kingdom of death. When you see its reality, it is already too late.

5

The Enemy of Man

The False Benefactor

Satan is hostile to God and to everything that is of God. Satan's hatred of man, the masterpiece of creation, is affirmed by Jesus Himself when he calls him, "murderer from the beginning" (John 8:44). Yet Satan's shrewdness in covering his perverse intentions is so great that some consider him a benefactor of humanity. Indeed, he manifests himself under this disguise at the moment of temptation.

Satan always has something in his hand to offer when he comes close to you. He is the greatest seller of false merchandise that exists. He studies your hunger and then presents to you the most alluring food. Do you want to have riches? He will show you easy money. Do you want power? He will show you the kingdoms of the world to take in your hand. Do you want success? He will indicate to you a secure shortcut. He knows the hunger for happiness that torments man, and he is most clever in making himself seem like the only one who can satisfy it.

It is impressive how the shrewd viper succeeds in deceiving even intelligent and cultured people with an ease that leaves one dismayed. Now, in this regard, I will allow myself to recount something I would not have believed had I not seen it personally. Many years ago, I met a girl who had attended the oratory until she was at the threshold of the university but who ceased to attend for professional and academic reasons. She told me that she had lost her faith after all those years and had become an atheist. I wanted to enter into a deeper conversation about faith with her, and she finally confessed to me of being tempted to sell her soul to Satan in order to make a name for herself in her career.

At that moment, I understood the subtle work the clever deceiver had placed in front of that soul. Having robbed her of God and prayer, Satan had shown her the mirage of a career as something to be reached at all costs. Once that desire had conquered the soul, killing all other values, he presented himself as the only one who could help her achieve it. I observed with bitter wonder that while some theologians cast into doubt the existence of Satan, he was in the shadows, buying the souls of the so-called atheists.

Satan presents himself to Adam as the one who can reveal to man the secret of becoming like God. To Christ he displays himself as the one who offers the solution to the problem of living and the one who can give man glory and unlimited power. If you think about it, the tempter never proposes the cross to you. The way he indicates to you is always easier and broader. He never ceases to hiss in your ear that the commandments of God are outdated, and he convinces you that you should enjoy the only life that you have to the utmost, savoring every instant granted to you.

Satan, the eternally unhappy, has no reluctance about presenting himself to men as the dispenser of happiness. They feed like fish on bait. Once they fall under his dominion by committing sin, they become aware of the tremendous deception. They deceived themselves into believing that they are happy; now they groan under the oppressive yoke of desperation, and it will not be easy for them to free themselves.

Jesus offers happiness also, but not as cheap merchandise. The evil one has fun convincing the foolish that the way of God is for fanatics. He insinuates to you that those who follow Jesus do not enjoy life. You can, however, always ask a person who follows God whether or not he is sorry for having chosen to do it. Now ask a person who has believed all of the promises of the tempter whether or not he is truly happy with his life. Satan wants to buy you at a cheap price, but Jesus has poured out His Blood in order to obtain your soul.

The Murderous Envy

The incomparable art of the great Florentine painter Masaccio has illustrated, in the immortal frescos of the Brancacci Chapel in Florence, the existential catastrophe provoked by the false promises of the great deceiver. It is perhaps the most ingenious and profound exegesis of Original Sin that has ever been presented in art.[3]

In the first panel, you see our first parents at the moment of temptation before they had sinned. Adam and Eve are still enwrapped by the splendor of the original creation, even though the shadow of evil has begun to touch them. Their bodies express all the beauty God the Creator has imprinted upon them. Eve, already persuaded by the words of the evil one, holds on to the tree of the knowledge of good and evil, as if she wants to make it her own. The serpent, who is hanging over her like a

[3] Masaccio adhered to the theory that the Original Sin was a sexual one. This theory is not officially taught by the Catholic Church.

dark menace, watches Adam while disguising his reptile head behind the fascination of Eve. The first woman looks at Adam intensely while she draws attention to herself. In this painting, the woman is the forbidden fruit Satan offers the man, disregarding the commandment of God.

It is a crucial moment when man is able to verify if it is possible to be happy in disobeying the commandments of the Creator. It is a test of truth in which he himself is able to measure the consistency of the great swindler's promises. In the next panel, Masaccio gives the unmistakable response. Our first parents are represented in the act of being cast out of the earthly paradise. Their bodies, bent under the weight of their fault, have lost their original splendor and demonstrate the gloominess of the flesh which has absorbed the poison of evil and has become subject to sickness, old age, and death. On their faces is depicted the infinite desperation of the human condition which each man experiences upon coming into the world.

Religious literature frequently recounts the extraordinary experience that many men have of passing from darkness to light, from sin to grace, and from slavery to evil to the freedom of the sons of God. It is the way of conversion which has found the highest and most moving expression in the parables of Jesus, especially in the parable of the prodigal son. Yet there is also an opposite way which many travel and which is useful to understand. It is that opposite way that leads one from good to evil, from joy to desperation, and from life to death. In no part of Scripture is this road that leads to self-destruction described with so much realism and efficacy as in the third chapter of Genesis.

Consider the condition of our first parents before sin. They were enjoying intimacy with God and a great communion between them and with nature. God, in His paternal love, had elevated man to the dignity of a friend, predestinating him to eternal life. Life here on earth should have taken place in great peace and serenity, without pain, suffering, evil, ignorance, death, or any evil thing that now afflicts the human condition. After a life full of joy and peace here on earth, men should have passed to the beatitude of Heaven.

Was not the life condition in which God placed our first parents happy? Yet they fell into the deception of Satan, hoping to have still more. In reality they lost everything, falling into a desperate condition for which they could find no remedy. Listening to the tempter, man finds himself without God and His friendship, although Providence never ceases to watch over man. Our first parents lost all the gifts they had received: from the gifts of immortality and of wisdom to the gifts of integrity and of the absence of pain. Our parents were especially deprived of the expectation of eternal life, from which they were excluded.

Now you understand why Jesus describes the devil as the one who is "a murderer from the beginning" (John 8:44). With great shrewdness, the evil one leads man to his death, seeking to nullify the Creator's projects of mercy. Satan has promised man an absolute freedom and independence, deceiving him into believing that he is able to emancipate himself from divine dependency. In reality, Satan has robbed man of everything, even his dignity, rendering man a slave to Satan's reign of death. To present God to you as an enemy and himself as a friend is the most insolent of his lies, yet men believe him.

The Art of Destruction

Satan seduces in order to destroy. His activity is the exact opposite of God's. If God is the Creator, then Satan is the destroyer. If God is life, then Satan is death. The biblical images of the roaring lion

(1 Pet. 5:8) and of the furious dragon (Rev. 12:3) express well the destructive violence of the evil one toward God's creation and, in particular, toward man. The violence has spread in the course of history, causing man to become like a wolf toward his fellow man. Reddening all the earth with blood would not be understandable without the poisonous hatred the serpent has injected into the veins of humanity.

What does the evil one destroy? First of all, he destroys individual persons. All of those who enter into the snare of his seduction are subordinated to a growing work of spiritual and moral disintegration. There is no man that Satan does not tempt toward evil. The spiritual combat is necessary for all those who desire to preserve themselves and to make progress on the way toward the good. Whoever does not struggle, committing oneself to the exercise of virtue, becomes prey to the evil one, who destroys all that God has built in the soul.

This work of spiritual devastation, which adults often succeed in covering under an external mask of decency, is particularly visible in young people. After they have received a religious education from their family and from their parish, discovering God and the practice of good, Satan succeeds in attracting them to himself with the multiple faces of the seductions of the world. Through ambiguous friendships and false teachers, he quickly deprives them of God, of the Faith, and of prayer. Then he pushes them toward the way of free sex, easy money, and pleasure.

After some months, these same youths are unrecognizable. Seduced by material things, they have lost the values that will guide them through life. Snuffed out at the spiritual level and degraded on the moral one, they have lost the ability to think about their own future. They live in an endless present and seek through fleeting pleasures to fill the existential emptiness that haunts them like a shadow. Continuing in this way, they end up breaking every moral limit, compromising their life in violence, theft, sexual disorder, alcohol, and drugs.

Look around and observe the shocking reality of so many youngsters whom the great seducer has led along the way of total ruin. They are destroyed lives which only the miracle of grace can heal through a long and arduous route of recovery.

The same activity of progressive destruction is untiringly carried forward against families. The devil divides, as the word in Greek itself states. His work of division begins with the fundamental cell of society, the family. His power of disintegration has produced impressive effects in this field. This is possible for him because more often than not, the young already present themselves to each other in matrimony spiritually empty. Their union being built on sand and not on the rock, it is a little game for the untiring devastator to destroy couples after only a few months of life in common.

As you see, dear friend, the evil one's work of destruction begins in every soul, passing through families and infiltrating society. He really does not need to toil very hard to bring society to moral shambles and total collapse. Indeed, a society is nothing other than the aggregation of the persons who compose it. When the majority of members of a social group are empty individuals, without ideals and without morality, Satan does not have difficulty in pushing this group toward violence, egoism, intolerance, and injustice. From here, it is a brief step to bring society to war and to the more brutal forms of destruction, even to the point of compromising the future of humanity and the existence of the world.

We must not have any illusions regarding Satan's will to destroy individuals as well as the whole of society. Certainly, his power and his freedom of action are subject to the power of God, who limits the evil one's sphere of action according to His wisdom. Nevertheless, God permits us to see with our eyes what the demon does to people who hand themselves over to him. Think of Judas and of his horrible end. The same end is often the final act in the life of one who has had faith in this false benefactor. Without coming to these extremes, observe the final end of those who have desired to go the way of ruin, deceiving themselves about having found happiness. Are not their lives empty, sad, and desperate?

To the Image of Satan

Satan seduces man, destroying all that is positive in him, in order to imprint in his soul "the mark of the beast" (see Rev. 13:16–18). Revelation on several occasions contrasts this mark to the "sign of the living God," with which the just are marked (see Rev. 22:4). What is this about?

The sign of the living God, which distinguishes the followers of the Lamb, is not so much an exterior sign as it is the attestation of an interior life. Every person who lives God's grace is inhabited by the Holy Trinity, who has made each one of them the temple of His glory. The soul in which God dwells is filled with His light, His peace, His joy, and His love. The divine presence shines on the face, in the gestures, in the words, and in the actions of a good person. Even in the fragility of the human condition here on earth, you see the living image of God shining in those people.

In the same way, although with a completely different meaning, the mark of the beast is not just a testimony of belonging to the evil one, who by sin has made us his slaves, but it is a manifestation of an interior presence of the dark one, who has taken possession of that heart which God had created for Himself and has made it his horrible lair. When the corruption of the soul has reached the bottom, Satan triumphantly enters into it, as he did with Judas (John 13:27). In this manner, he completes the work of molding you to his image.

Do not think that this is an exaggeration. The possession of the heart, obdurate in evil, is infinitely more common than the possession of the body. St. Catherine of Siena did not hesitate to call impenitent sinners "incarnate demons," by whom Satan serves himself through his nefarious work in the world.

When a person hates God and blasphemes Him, voluntarily putting himself at the evil one's service in the untiring activity of the spiritual and moral disintegration of society, has he not transformed himself from the image of God into the image of the evil one? Satan repays his own, giving himself as the reward. For those who imitate him, "the cowardly, the faithless, the polluted, as for murderers, fornicators, sorcerers, idolaters, and all liars, their lot shall be in the lake that burns with fire and brimstone" (Rev. 21:8), where the devil and his own will be tormented for ever and ever (Rev. 20:10).

6

The Prince of This World

The Right of Conquest

Satan is strong. Each of us experiences Satan's strength personally at the moment of temptation and in the obstacles he puts on the road to salvation. The Church has full awareness of it in her difficult navigation through the two millennia of her history, among the persecutions, storms, and traps by which Satan has sought to overcome her. The world confirms it, because it is still largely under his influence, in spite of the victory achieved by Christ, who by His Passion "delivered us from Satan and sin" (CCC 1708).

We can have no doubts about the strength of the devil. It would be enough to meditate on the book of Revelation to realize the ability of the dragon to destroy and to seduce men even after the Redemption. His activity knows no rest. It can be clearly seen throughout all human history, and it will become more intense and furious in the times preceding the end. Jesus recognizes the reality of this perverse demon when He calls him "the ruler of this world" (John 12:31; 14:30; 16:11).

We are the protagonists in this great battle against the evil one, in which we struggle for the eternal salvation of our souls. It is essential to know the origin of his power as well as the spheres within which he works so that we may have the possibility of defeating him. It would be a mistake to overestimate him, as if the enemy could do everything he wants. He is strong but not omnipotent. Likewise, it would be dangerous to underestimate him, as even our first parents, who were clothed in grace, wisdom, and the strength of God, were deceived and conquered.

It is important to underline that at the beginning of human history, Satan achieved a great victory whose consequences will be felt by all the descendants of Adam until the end of time. Through Original Sin, the devil has obtained a right of dominion over all mankind. Every child who is born is under the influence of the evil one. "By our first parents' sin, the devil has acquired a certain domination over man, even though man remains free. Original sin entails 'captivity under the power of him who thenceforth had the power of death, that is, the devil'" (CCC 407).

The Redemption worked by Christ does not prevent that children will be born with the sin of Adam, and because of this fact, they are under the influence of the evil one. For this reason, we need to give them the sacrament of Baptism, through which the child is liberated from sin and from its instigator, the devil. This is shown by the exorcisms which are pronounced over the candidate (child or adult), by whose power Satan is explicitly renounced (CCC 1237).

The effects of Baptism, which clothe us with sanctifying grace, are admirable. Baptism raises us to the dignity of sons of God, makes us members of the Church which is the Body of Christ, and opens to us the doors of eternal life. Yet there still remain in us some painful traces of the original evil. The Church teaches that even after the sacrament of Baptism, "the consequences for nature, weakened and inclined to evil, persist in man and summon him to spiritual battle" (CCC 405).

Concupiscence, which lives in our members, as is magisterially taught by St. Paul, in itself is not sin but pushes men toward sin. This is the consequence of Satan's victory over our first parents, and the shrewd serpent knows how to exploit it to his advantage to freely induce us to evil and to make us his own with our consent. In His wisdom, God permits this so that, with the help of His grace, we can achieve merit and the crown of victory.

The World under the Power of the Evil One

Is the initial victory of Satan over our first parents enough to explain the great power that the evil one has over this world? The sin of Eden should not be minimized, neither in itself nor in the grave consequences it had on humanity. It was a true spiritual catastrophe, since by it "man *preferred* himself to God and by that very act scorned him. He chose himself over and against God, against the requirements of his creaturely status and therefore against his own good. Constituted in a state of holiness, man was destined to be fully 'divinized' by God in glory. Seduced by the devil, he wanted to 'be like God,' but 'without God, before God, and not in accordance with God'" (CCC 398).

Man's gesture of rebellion was similar to that of the rebellious angels, even though it was not as irreversible and immutable as theirs because of the limits of human nature. Through Adam and Eve, humanity has chosen the road proposed by Satan, abandoning God and His grace. Of course, man has maintained in himself the capacity to do good, albeit with a weakened freedom. Having fallen by his own free will under the influence of the evil one, he easily cedes to Satan's suggestions, movements, and deceptions.

If you meditate on the history of humanity from the expulsion from the earthly paradise to the universal deluge (Gen. 4–7), you will realize that it is presented in the Bible in very negative terms, as a process of moral and spiritual degradation in which sexual perversion and violence fully feed the flooding river of evil and of sin. When the Creator takes stock of the situation of humanity, the balance is disastrous: "The Lord saw that the wickedness of man was great in the earth, and that every imagination of the thoughts of his heart was only evil continually. And the Lord was sorry that he had made man on the earth, and it grieved him to his heart. So the Lord said, 'I will blot out man whom I have created from the face of the ground, man and beast and creeping things and birds of the air, for I am sorry that I have made them.'" (Gen. 6:5–7).

After the deluge, the situation did not improve. Even with the particular election of the people of Israel, there is no return to God. The word of the prophets is a saddened call to conversion which runs throughout the entire history of salvation until it culminates in the strong and powerful preaching of John the Baptist. Does not Jesus Himself begin His mission with a peremptory invitation to change one's life? "Repent and believe in the gospel" are the first public words to come out of His mouth (Mark 1:15).

Do you realize that the vision of human history offered in the Word of God, from Original Sin until the coming of the Savior, is prevalently negative? Of course, here and there lights of sanctity and the small flock of those who remain faithful to God can be found, testifying that goodness is possible. Nevertheless, the world as a whole multiplies its sins, becoming more and more a slave to the evil one. Do not think that the coming of the Redeemer coincides with a moment of particular spiritual fervor in the history of mankind. Quite to the contrary, He has come as a sun from on high in order to illuminate a world which lies "in darkness and in the shadow of death" (Luke 1:79).

When Jesus affirms that Satan is the prince of this world, He only reveals the empire of evil that the dark one had surreptitiously constructed for himself over the course of history, occupying the minds and hearts of men and infiltrating society and its institutions. Jesus casts new light on the vastness of evil, revealing the hidden director, but especially He affirms that with His coming, the great battle to free a world that lies under the dominion of the evil one has begun (1 John 5:19).

Now you will wonder how it happened that Satan succeeded in acquiring such a thorough and deep hold over humanity to be able to challenge the Messiah, telling Him that all the kingdoms of the world are in his hands (Luke 4:6). Here we are confronted by a very delicate theological problem, which should be clarified immediately. Satan's power is certainly great, but he is not in a position to bend the human will. If he obtained victory over our first parents and has become the ruler of this world, it is because men allowed themselves to be blinded by his seductions and have chosen evil instead of good. This was true even before the Redemption, because God did not withhold His help from those who turned to Him, but it is especially true after the Redemption, when the Christian in union with Christ can, if he wants, succeed in evading all of the serpent's snares.

Satan Is Subject to God

At times, observing the devastation of demonic action against people and society, we spontaneously cry with the psalmist, "How long, Lord?" We are shocked and dismayed by the undeniable successes of the evil one, especially those he has achieved after the Redemption. At times, there is a temptation toward discouragement in seeing evil triumph over good. This is true especially in our time, which is experiencing, in a quiet way, one of the most serious and grave apostasies in recorded Christian history. Nor are the prospects for the future rose-colored, because the final phase of history will not conclude with the triumph of the Church but rather with its greatest persecution and with its attempted destruction by the forces of evil (CCC 677).

We do not doubt that the power of the demon is great, at least as great as his hatred. Nevertheless, his power depends in great part on men, who support it with their acceptance of evil and of sin. The force of Satan is fed by our free will, and this is certainly the most sorrowful aspect of the problem. Since many men prefer the devil to God, we are confronted by a dark mystery of folly and of seduction. The great deceiver often succeeds in making himself seem preferable to God. This explains very well his power over the world.

Nevertheless, God could have relegated Satan to Hell at the very beginning, without permitting him to move about the earth. Satan's power of seduction, of temptation, of placing obstacles, of persecuting, and of waging war depends on divine permission. The dragon may only act with force in the places, in the times, and in the ways in which God allows. He is a creature, and if God did not sustain his existence, he would fall into nothingness. However, in the spheres of divine permission, he acts without rest, exploiting every situation to hamper the plans of God and to build his reign of death as an eternal challenge to the Creator.

Do Satan's successes constitute a defeat for God? This is a difficult question to answer, at least here on earth. It would be like asking if Hell represents a stain in the design of Divine Mercy. Certainly God suffers for the souls who fall into damnation and for whom the incarnate Son has suffered unto death to bring salvation. Yet even they, in their own way, render testimony to the infinite wisdom of the Creator, who has desired to give the immense gift of freedom to His creatures.

The nefarious activity the evil one is able to exercise until the end of time can be enormous, but nonetheless, his power is "not infinite. He is only a creature, powerful from the fact that he is pure spirit, but still a creature. He cannot prevent the building up of God's reign. Although Satan may act in the world out of hatred for God and his kingdom in Christ Jesus, and although his action may cause grave injuries—of a spiritual nature and, indirectly, even of a physical nature—to each man and to society, the action is permitted by divine providence which with strength and gentleness guides human and cosmic history. It is a great mystery that providence should permit diabolical activity, but 'we know that in everything God works for good with those who love him'" (CCC 395).

Man Remains Free

Something funny occurs to me, even in such a serious and dramatic context: Satan has become the prince of this world in a rather democratic way. It is true that he has used deception, showing evil under the form of good to our first parents, but they were able to understand and to decide freely what they wanted. Their minds were illuminated by the Divine Wisdom, their wills were immune to the injuries of sin and clothed by the gift of strength. If they sinned, harking to the demon instead of God, they did it with full warning and with deliberate consent. It is man who has crowned Satan as the lord of the world.

It is man who sustains the kingdom of darkness, voluntarily handing himself over to sin. Certainly, man is weaker after the Fall, and Satan takes advantage of this condition; but after the Redemption, we have every weapon necessary to combat him and defeat him. Nevertheless, we see him opposing the kingship of Christ with untamed ferocity. Why is this possible? Because men want it. Satan cannot make us his own if we do not consent. He can render us slaves of his kingdom of darkness only if we say yes to evil.

St. Thomas Aquinas makes a very illuminating observation: that both Satan and the good angels, inasmuch as they are more intelligent and powerful than men, can exercise some influence on us, but not in such a manner as to deprive us of our free will. Both Satan and the good angels, although with opposite objectives, can influence our external senses, our imaginations, our fantasies, and even our minds. The good angels do it to stimulate us toward good, while Satan and the rebellious angels do it to lead us toward evil. Nevertheless, neither Satan nor the good angels can bend the human will, since to do so belongs exclusively to God.

God alone, with His grace, can infallibly move the will toward good, yet maintaining its freedom. This is a mystery which the greatest Christian minds have sought to fathom, but for us it is enough to know the simplicity of its formulation. You alone are master of your free will, and even when God intervenes with His efficacious grace, obtaining the desired effects, your will continues to be free.

If man does not want to, he does not sin. When you adhere to sin with free consent and foolishly yet voluntarily go forward on the way of ruin, your will becomes enslaved to sin, as Jesus Himself emphasized, "Every one who commits sin is a slave to sin" (John 8:34). In this case, your free will is as dead. Only a completely gratuitous and unmerited grace can awaken it and sustain it on the way of rebirth. It is through the grace of conversion that God instills life in your will and with your collaboration strengthens it, bringing it one step at a time along the way of salvation.

God can bend the human will, Satan cannot. This is a sure truth of the Faith that gives us great consolation. The citizens of the kingdom of death belong to it because they desire it. They could depart at any moment, if only they would cooperate with the grace of the true Prince of this world.

7

The Victory of Christ

The Prophecy of Eden

Any statement on the demon would be misleading if the victory of Christ were not strongly underlined. Although Satan has won a battle, Christ has won the war. Inasmuch as the "great dragon" is infuriated and has the capacity to seduce the whole earth (Rev. 12:9), we should not forget that "by his passion, Christ delivered us from Satan and from sin" (CCC 1708). This does not mean that the evil one no longer has the possibility to cause harm. On the contrary, as an injured beast, he is even more dangerous than before. Knowing that the allotted time is limited, he exploits every useful occasion, and he does not allow himself a moment of rest. Nevertheless, the situation has now radically changed, because after the Redemption, man has received from God the light to discover the snares of the enemy and the strength given by grace to resist his assaults and achieve the victory.

Any attempt to minimize the victory of Christ over Satan should be considered as a very subtle diabolical snare. There are those who justify sin by saying that man's inclination toward evil is invincible. Today, many sins are excused—if not theoretically, at least in fact—by man's refusal to set them in the light, covering them instead with a blanket of oblivion. An example that comes to mind is the leaving aside in habitual preaching of everything regarding many sexual sins. St. John the Baptist was beheaded for having denounced a sin of adultery. The first Christian community considered this sin to be the gravest after apostasy and homicide. Nowadays, it is simply not spoken about? Why?

We wonder what is the deep root of a certain acceptance of evil by many Christians of our time. At times, they seem like an army retreating in disorder, having fallen prey to discouragement and tacitly resigned to defeat. Evil seems to triumph and sing of victory. Satan's tactic is to frighten us with his successes to make us throw in the towel before we fight. Exterior appearances seem to show that he is right. Are not large parts of society under his influence, especially in the most important sectors? Politics, economics, the mass media, and culture are, to a large extent, in his hands. However, his strength compared to God's power is just a false strength. Believers must never forget that the little sling of David was enough to knock down the giant Goliath.

The victory of Christ over Satan is the heart of the Gospel. It has inaugurated the new time of grace and mercy. The boat of Peter is unsinkable, no matter how much the gates of Hell seek to prevail (Matt. 16:18). With the Redemption, Christ becomes the master of history. He is the powerful One who has bound Beelzebub, snatching the prey from him (Matt. 12:29). Even though the book of Revelation prophetically describes the impressive unleashing of the power of evil at the end of the world, in reality the Victor over the strength and power of the beast is the Lamb, the King of kings, and the Lord of lords (Rev. 17:14). He is the true Prince of this world, not Satan.

From the moment of the ancient serpent's victory, God made it clear that it was a temporary triumph and that One would come who would crush his head: "I will put enmity between you and the woman, and between your seed and her seed: he shall bruise your head, and you shall bruise his heel" (Gen. 3:15). All history preceding Christ is illuminated by this great prophecy of liberation and victory. Before the Redemption, humanity saw the expansion of the power of darkness, but there always remained the hope of liberation. The dominion of Satan over the world has never been secure. In spite of the expansion of evil, God has always had His friends, and the light of truth has shone in consciences and was never extinguished, even in the darkest moments. This has enabled men not to lose the way completely and has allowed them to receive in every period of history the necessary help for salvation.

Christ the New Adam

Jesus Christ is the victor over sin, evil, and death because He has triumphed over Satan. The Gospels overflow with this victory, which is already evident in the public life of Jesus when the demons are forced to come out into the open by the splendor of His light and to flee terrified at the command of His word. His public life is opened with Satan's own assault. The ancient adversary knows that he has in front of him the Seed of the Woman of whom the prophecy speaks. Satan approaches the New Adam, not withholding anything from his power of seduction. He realizes that if he does not win, his ruin is close. He withdraws, defeated, while he meditates on a different and more ferocious plot. When he does not prevail with the weapon of seduction, Satan, full of rage, seeks to destroy. But in the meantime, the kingdom of evil shakes for the first time and topples down to its foundations: a filthy demon cries, "Ah! What have you to do with us, Jesus of Nazareth? Have you come to destroy us? I know who you are, the Holy One of God" (Luke 4:34).

The victory of Christ over Satan and over his kingdom of death is the basic theme of the New Testament. Jesus affirms without hesitation that the proof that the Reign of God is now present is shown by the fact that the demons are driven away and men are freed (Mark 3:22–30). But what is the fundamental reason that the coming of Christ begins the destruction of the reign of evil? The answer is found in the very mystery of the Person of Jesus. If the New Adam were only a man, Satan would not have much to fear. Had not the ancient serpent defeated the first Adam when he was in the splendor of his sanctity? But the ruin of Satan and his empire of evil is found in the very coming of God to earth.

Jesus is the Word of God made Man. Satan is not confronting a simple man but the God-Man. He can do nothing against Him. Satan's defeat began at the moment of the Incarnation. Through Mary, the Word is made flesh, and the Kingdom of God plants its roots on the earth. It is the beginning of the end for the powers of Hell. Certainly, blinded by an unlimited pride, the prince of this world plans to seduce even the Son of God and comes to request adoration from Him (Matt. 4:9). The one who had challenged God in Heaven (Rev. 12:7) does not hesitate to challenge Him here on earth, but Satan's defeat is secure. It proceeds in an inexorable way until the end of history, when the Son of man will pronounce the definitive sentence: "depart from me, you cursed, into the eternal fire prepared for the devil and his angels" (Matt. 25:41).

God having realized from all eternity the hidden plan of sending His Son to earth (Col. 1:26), the victory over the prince of this world is an irrevocable event. The single fact that God Himself has been made man is the end for Satan. What can the creature, however intelligent and powerful, do against his

Creator? Less than nothing. You see this in the confrontations between Jesus and the demons documented in the Gospels. The disciples are amazed that in the name of Jesus they are able to cast out demons. They express their amazement: "Even the demons are subject to us in your name" (Luke 10:17). In reality, it is the power of Christ which acts, that is, the strength of God Himself.

Jesus, dear friend, is not holy but is Holiness; He is not wise but is Wisdom; He is not strong but is Strength; He is not luminous but is the Light; He is not potent but is Omnipotence. His Gospel is not a human word but is the Word of God. When Jesus advances, Satan moves backward. This truth is valid also for the Church, which is the prolongation of Christ, and it applies to every Christian who is a member of His Body and a temple of the Holy Spirit. If the Word Himself has been made flesh and has dwelt in our midst (John 1:14), manifesting His glory, full of grace and truth, will He not overcome the kingdom of evil and of lies? If the Raised One remains with us until the end of the world (Matt. 28:20), how will the power of sin and of death be able to impose itself? Confronting the great uproar made by evil and its apparent victories, believers must never lose faith. We, like Paul, when among the greatest dangers, can and must say: "If God is for us, who is against us?" (Rom. 8:31).

The Great Duel

The struggle between Christ and Satan in the desert marks the beginning of Jesus' public life, which opens with the victory of the New Adam over the ancient tempter. However, the match is not over. The evangelist Luke notes this, affirming that the devil, having exhausted every kind of temptation, withdrew from Jesus in order to return at "an opportune time" (Luke 4:13).

The decisive moment of the struggle is at the very end of Jesus' life, which closes with His apparent defeat. Luke reports the words of Jesus at the tragic moment of Gethsemane. The Master invites the three disciples who are with Him to stay awake and to pray not to fall into temptation while He, prey to the great agony, sweats Blood and begs the Father, if it may be possible, to take away the bitter chalice of the Passion.

The climate is one of great oppression. A sense of impending evil hangs over Jesus like a great weight. The supreme effort of His soul to resist the greatest satanic storm that has ever been set loose results in the sweat of Blood. There are moments in which the empire of darkness assaults the soul with anguish, tremors, fears, and frights that are impossible to describe but that have been well understood by those saints who have had the rare grace of experiencing them.

In those tremendous situations, the soul feels abandoned by God while she sees rising up around her a deep wave of evil, which seems to swallow her. Who can know what Jesus experienced on the Mount of Olives? The merciful Father sent an angel from Heaven to comfort Him (Luke 22:43). Perhaps the apostles' abandonment of Him and the wavering of their faith was weighing Him down. In all likelihood, Satan had shown Him the failure of His mission, and as proof, he scornfully placed in front of Him Judas, who betrayed Him with the most disgraceful kiss in the history of humanity. If we remember that at that moment the betrayer was inhabited by Satan in person (John 13:27), then we can imagine the effort that Jesus had to make in addressing Judas as "dear friend."

What did the evil one not engineer in those hours to discourage the soul of Jesus, to break His heart, and to make Him admit His defeat? Never as on that night has the kingdom of evil manifested its monstrous strength—oppression, anguish, despondency, as well as feelings of emptiness, of failure, and of uselessness. Some mystical souls suggest that the great deceiver insinuated that the Passion would be useless, because man would continue to prefer him, that is, to prefer Satan to the Son of God. Look at his demonstration: for love of men, the Word of God made Himself man, but men advanced with swords and clubs to capture Him like a brigand. "This is your hour, and the power of darkness," exclaims Jesus (Luke 22:53).

It is an uncontestable biblical affirmation that the Passion represents the gravest satanic offensive against Christ. Luke (22:3, 31, 53) and John (13:2, 27; 6:70) especially affirm this. This is the conviction of the first Christian communities, to which the apostle Paul refers: "We impart a secret and hidden wisdom of God, which God decreed before the ages for our glorification. None of the rulers of this age understood this; for if they had, they would not have crucified the Lord of glory" (1 Cor. 2:7–8).

In other words, Satan (the ruler of this world) did not realize that eliminating Jesus through the infamy of the Cross would assist the divine design of the Redemption. God, in His mysterious wisdom, used the plan of Satan to defeat him definitively and break his dominion over man.

How was this possible? It happened because of the total obedience and submission of Jesus to the will of the Father. Initially, Satan sought with all his strength to prevent Jesus from drinking the chalice of suffering. He surrounded Him with the terrors of death (Ps. 55:5) so that Jesus would experience a mortal sadness: "My soul is very sorrowful, even to death" (Mark 14:34). Then the evil one sought to avert Christ's baptism of blood (Luke 12:50), which was by now imminent; but Jesus responded by renewing His total abandonment to the will of His Father: "Abba, Father, all things are possible to thee; remove this cup from me; yet not what I will, but what thou wilt" (Mark 14:36).

So it happened that Satan hurled himself against Jesus with unimaginable ferocity even until His final breath on the Cross, but the Lamb of God let Himself be led to the slaughter as a victim of love to redeem the world. When the destructive wrath of the adversary of God brought to completion the heinous crime, the work of the Redemption was complete. Hatred was defeated by love, and pride by the humble submission and heroism of the Son to the will of the Father. The one who had triumphed, attracting the first man to the tree of the knowledge of good and evil, was mortally wounded by the New Adam, whom he had nailed to the tree of the Cross.

"Yours Is the Kingdom and the Power"

By dying on the Cross and imploring the Father's pardon on humanity, Christ freed us from the power of the prince of this world and established His Kingdom on earth. The evil one was not able to do anything against Him (John 14:30). On the eve of the Passion, Jesus had predicted: "Now shall the ruler of this world be cast out" (John 12:31). At the beginning of Jesus' ministry, Satan had dared to offer Him the dominion of the world (Luke 4:6), claiming that it belonged to him by right of conquest after the victory in Eden. But after the Passion and His glorious Resurrection, the scepter of the world belongs to Christ alone. Sending the apostles, He says, "All authority in heaven and on earth has been given to me. Go therefore, and make disciples of all nations ... lo, I am with you always, to the close of the age" (Matt. 28:18–20).

Before the victorious Lord, every knee must bend "in heaven and on earth and under the earth" (Phil. 2:10). Even the empire of evil and its dark prince are subject to the power of Jesus. The history of the world is firmly in His hands, and even evil is forced to cooperate with the glory of God.

Although the "roaring lion" is on an untiring quest for whom he may devour (1 Pet. 5:8), he is not able to cause harm if man does not acquiesce. Although Satan's work of seduction and persecution is full of snares, man can defeat the evil one with the grace of Christ. Clothed in "the armor of God" (Eph. 6:11), the Christian is invincible. The time allotted to Satan until the end of the world is to allow man to ransom himself, combating Satan and defeating him. God does not leave additional space and time to the devil for taking hold of our souls but to allow us with Christ to humiliate him, crushing his proud head.

8

The Powerful Virgin against Evil

"I Will Put Enmity between You and the Woman"

The one who has defeated the empire of evil is Jesus Christ. His victory, which began at the moment of the Incarnation, was realized during the great test of the Passion and was manifested in all the splendor of His glory on the day of Easter. The Divine Wisdom allows Satan to act until the end of the world to associate the Church and every Christian with the combat and victory of Christ.

Now we must seek to comprehend the place of the Virgin Mary in this dramatic duel which runs through all of human history. The faith of the simple Christian assigns to the Virgin, who is powerful against evil, a decisive role in the fight against Satan. Very often in the common thinking of the faithful, it is held that the Virgin, more so than Christ, has the task of crushing Satan's head. Are we confronted here by some exaggeration, or has the supernatural instinct of the people simply grasped a precious aspect of revealed truth?

We should keep very much in mind an essential and irremovable aspect of the work of the Redemption completed by Christ, that it is realized with the intimate, constant, and fundamental collaboration of the Virgin Mary. Divine Wisdom has decided that the woman, the New Eve, should be placed side by side with the New Adam in the struggle against Satan for the liberation of humanity. If Christ is the Redeemer, the Virgin Mary is the co-redeemer.[4] From the moment of the Incarnation until Christ's death on the Cross, the Mother is beside the Son and shares each moment of the deadly conflict.

It is incomprehensible that some wish to separate the Mother from the Son, seeking to relegate her to the shadows, making her task seem insignificant. The two evocative biblical impressions of the tremendous battle between God and Satan, that of Genesis (3:15) and that of the book of Revelation (12:1–6), join the woman to the Son as if they were almost a single thing.

In particular, we are surprised by the luminous prophecy placed at the beginning of human history as a sign of hope for the future liberation. It is affirmed, it is true, that it will be not the woman but her seed that will crush the head of the serpent. Can we doubt that Christ is the One who has torn away the scepter from the prince of the kingdom of evil? Certainly not, but He is the seed of Mary, and not just in the biological sense. Indeed, He was born of a woman of whom it is asserted that she is the irreducible enemy of the infernal serpent.

When God declares, "I will put enmity between you and the woman" (Gen. 3:15), He says something extremely profound which is to be understood in all of its immense meaning. In the divine disposition of salvation, a rebellious creature, who has

[4] When speaking of the Blessed Virgin Mary as collaborating with Christ in the Redemption, it is important to understand that she collaborates with Him as a subordinate, not as an equal. Everything that Mary does is intimately connected to Christ, her Son, and she subordinates her will to the Father as the handmaid of the Lord.

dragged humanity to ruin through the collaboration of a woman, confronts another creature, also a woman. She instead is submissive and faithful, and her duty is to humiliate the proud one, tearing away from him the souls redeemed by the Blood of the Son.

This underlining of the enmity of the New Eve toward Satan emphasizes the fundamental role God assigns to Mary in the struggle against the evil one. She not only cooperates with the victory of the Son but also carries out through divine disposition a specific mission in the tearing away from Satan every single soul that God has entrusted to her maternal solicitude. Who is more determined, intransigent, and untiring than a mother when it concerns the salvation of her own child? In her maternal heart, Mary find finds the most profound reason to hold enmity toward the devil. She does not permit Satan to bring to ruin the souls that Christ has entrusted to her, and for this she resists with all the power that Christ has given to her.

"From the First Instant"

By divine decision, the New Eve, Mother of the new generation of the living, is the irreducible enemy of Satan and, together with the Savior, has the task of defeating Satan and crushing his head. The pride of the rebellious angel is given a deadly blow from the moment in which God makes use of a creature, and in particular, a woman, to realize the plan of redemption entrusted to His Son.

Satan has other and no less important reasons for nourishing a particular hatred against Mary. In this regard, it is interesting to report the testimony of exorcist priests, who agree that when the name of Mary is pronounced, a person possessed or disturbed by a demon manifests the most violent reactions.

What is the reason for this? It is necessary to add another reason, which is certainly not secondary, to the reasons already given. Mary is the only creature on whom Satan has not exercised, even for an instant, his right of conquest. Beginning with our first parents, all the creatures who are derived from them, until the end of the world, carry in themselves the sign of the bite of the ancient serpent, which is transmitted through Original Sin. No man can claim to be exempt from that tremendous slavery of evil into which we are born.

Mary is the only exception. The one who is Full of Grace is the only human person who, from the moment of her conception, has been preserved from Original Sin. In calling Mary the "All Holy," the Church affirms that the one who was predestined to divine maternity had been conceived in the splendor of grace from the first instant. This means that Satan has never been able to claim any right over her. Mary has always been completely and solely of God. This is the profound reason for her enmity toward the serpent and the reason for the uncontrollable fury of the evil one at the mere sound of her name.

I would like to underline the importance of the expression "from the first instant," which Bl. Pope Pius IX specifically willed should be included in the formulation of the dogma of the Immaculate Conception. In the debate that preceded this dogmatic definition, and which lasted more than a millennium, there were some theologians who were so concerned about upholding the truth of the Faith regarding the universality of Original Sin that they affirmed that, at least in the instant of her conception, the Virgin Mary had contracted Original Sin, only to be healed of it immediately afterward through a special grace, in view of her future divine maternity.

Whenever this hypothesis was proposed in preaching, it was met with the hostility of the Christian people, who would often expel from the Church the so-called "maculate" preachers, that is, those who maintained that the one Full of Grace had been conceived "stained" (Latin *macula*) by Original Sin. The supernatural instinct of the faithful would not accept that Satan could claim possession over Mary, even at the first instant of her conception.

The great controversy ended in 1854 with the solemn proclamation of the dogma of the Immaculate Conception "from the first instant of conception," meaning that the enmity between the serpent and the woman was total and radical. The evil one was never able to touch her even slightly, not even for a moment. Four years later, at Lourdes, when St. Bernadette asked Mary her name, the Virgin Mary affirmed her title as the Immaculate Conception.

Certainly we have here an extraordinary and enormous gift of grace, given to Mary in view of the merits of Jesus Christ. This means that Our Lady has been redeemed, but in a way much more perfect than us, inasmuch as the grace of redemption has been offered to her from the first instant. She who was going to generate the victor over the evil one was never subject to Satan. To whom, if not to her, the woman clothed with the sun of divine sanctity, could Jesus have entrusted the task of tearing souls away from the furious dragon who wants to devour them?

"Blessed Is She Who Believed"

Now comes a great question to which it is not easy to respond. From the beginning of Jesus' public life, Satan drew closer to Jesus to tempt Him with every kind of temptation, as the evangelist Luke observed. We know that the satanic assault was resumed particularly at the moment of the Passion to avert the Messiah from fulfilling the will of the Father and to render useless the work of the Redemption. Is it possible to conjecture that Mary also had to confront the demon's seductions and persecutions during her life?

The Word of God does not reveal much to us in this regard, but it is possible nevertheless to make some fruitful reflections based on known truths of the Faith. First and foremost, it is necessary to grasp in its entire scope the expression with which the angel saluted the Virgin of Nazareth at the moment of the Annunciation. He calls her "Full of Grace," as if this were her proper name. It is a total fullness, as many exegetes have observed correctly, which not only excludes Original Sin but also any form, even minimal, of personal sin. In other words, Mary is clothed with a sanctity so sublime that it is impossible to find even the smallest imperfection in her soul.

The eminent sanctity of Mary, a mystery that cannot be fully comprehended here on earth, is at the same time both an extraordinary gift of grace as well as her perfect and free correspondence to that gift. Mary has "become holy," in the sense that she brought to full maturity the seeds of sanctity that the Holy Spirit had poured out in her. Her life on earth left a perfume of holiness that the great dragon could not miss. He knew well the ancient prophecy that joined the women and her offspring to the great battle in which he would be defeated. It is, therefore, absolutely logical to think that if Satan did not hesitate to tempt the New Adam, the same would apply to the New Eve.

Although the Word of God is reserved regarding this, there are nevertheless small but precious openings of light. The most important account is without any doubt the text of the book of Revelation, which evokes the grandiose celestial sign of the woman clothed with the sun, opposed by an enormous red dragon who attempts to devour the baby to whom she is about to give birth (Rev. 12:1–6). The common opinion of the exegetes is that the woman evoked by John is at the same time both the Virgin Mary and the Church. Both, making an inseparable reality, are made objects of persecution by the dragon, "that ancient serpent, who is called the Devil and Satan, the deceiver of the whole world" (Rev. 12:9).

Mary, like Jesus, certainly suffered from the persecutions and temptations of Satan here on earth. Is it possible to offer some plausible hypotheses regarding the immediate temptations brought by the evil one against the Virgin Mary? We can affirm, through an evident analogy of faith, that Mary, like Jesus (Luke 4:13), had been subject to every kind of temptation. She who cooperated with the Son in the work of redemption shared with Him also the great battles. Is it possible to single out a particular moment of Mary's personal struggle against the prince of evil?

Consider the analogy between the tree of the knowledge of good and evil and the tree of the Cross, which the Fathers of the Church have also emphasized. Eve, at the foot of the tree of Eden, listened to the poisonous words of the serpent, who filled her heart with disbelief and distrust of God. The sin of our first parents, even before being an act of pride and disobedience, was an attitude of disbelief and lack of faith in their Creator (CCC 397).

What did the ancient serpent hiss to the heart of Mary as she was standing at the foot of the tree of the Cross? We can think that even in this moment, he sought to insinuate thoughts of distrust, lack of faith, disbelief, and perhaps even rebellion against the Divine Goodness and Wisdom. There was the Son nailed to the Cross. The world had rejected Him, the apostles had abandoned Him, and the celestial Father seemed to remain silent. Under the darkened sky of that holy Friday, in the satanic darkness that enshrouded everything, the New Eve fought the great battle of faith, and through it, together with the crucified Son, she defeated the dark prince of this world.[5]

"Behold, Your Mother"

A question spontaneously arises regarding the profound motivation of the eminent sanctity with which God has clothed the New Eve, taking away from her even the smallest influence of the serpent. The fundamental reason for this is certainly the divine maternity. She who would become the Ark of the New Covenant and the Mother of the Incarnate Word could certainly not be exposed to even the smallest imperfection. Associated with the Thrice Holy One in the struggle against the evil one, she had to be necessarily "All Holy."

Mary is not only the Mother of the Head but also of the entire mystical Body. Her maternity is extended to all the brothers of her Son until the end of the world. In the same way that she has cooperated with the Son in the victory over Satan, by divine disposition, she is close to every man in the great spiritual warfare, in which eternal life is at stake.

The Divine Wisdom has established that Satan will remain active, with the ability to seduce and to tempt, until the conclusion of history. This freedom of action has not been granted to him so that souls may be lost. Christ has put His Mother next to every man so that he can achieve victory and the crown of glory. Who could help us more than she in the daily warfare against the evil one?

As all the children of Eve are born under the influence of the evil one, so all the children of Mary are freed and saved. The

[5] I have developed this subject in my book: *Magnificat, Il Poema di Maria* (Milan: Sugarco Edizioni, 1999), Canto XIII.

Virgin, powerful against evil, does not substitute for Jesus Christ in the struggle against Satan, but rather her maternal love is the victorious weapon which the Savior has made available to us. When Jesus, looking at St. John from the Cross, gives him Mary as Mother, He offers to every man an invincible weapon against the empire of darkness.

There is no doubt that Mary carries out her maternal task in a perfect way. Only in Heaven will we understand how much her help and protection have been decisive in foiling the vast shrewdness of the serpent. Who can know from how many dangers this admirable Mother has saved us, without our being aware? Mary is always Mother to us, even when we are far away from her through indifference and sin.

Nevertheless, if we receive her in our life and entrust to her our journey of sanctity, we can be assured that no snare of the serpent will be able to harm us, no seduction will lead us astray, and no bite will be mortal. Satan used a woman to condemn humanity; Jesus Christ avails Himself of the woman to lead souls to salvation.

9

The Tempter

Satan Tempts Man toward Evil

The activity of Satan is manifold. His goal is to abduct souls from God to make them eternally his own in his kingdom of death. Although defeated by the Cross of Christ, the devil maintains all his treachery and is even more aggressive and untiring than before, since he knows that the time allotted to him is short (Rev. 12:12). Now that believers are provided with the weapons of light for fighting and defeating him, the infuriated dragon pulls out from the depths of the abyss new and unknown forms of seduction and aggression. His fury will reach its zenith in the end times, when Hell will unfold its maximum power before its definitive defeat (2 Thess. 2:8).

Today, the devil is often spoken of, at least on a popular level, in order to point out physical disturbances in the cases of some illnesses or to explore some unusual manifestations in the cases of possession. The prayer of liberation from less serious phenomena and the prayer of exorcism for graver ones are requested with an increased frequency by the faithful.

It would be erroneous to limit the activity of Satan, solely or principally, to such a restricted sphere. There is no doubt that Jesus exercised His power of command on the demon, driving Satan from the possessed and even from some who were sick, as is clear from numerous evangelical testimonies; but the whole teaching of Scripture warns us about many other assaults, much more insidious, against which the faithful are often found disarmed.

First and foremost is the sowing of hatred between men. Satan, although a creature, is in a certain sense the anti-god. If God is love, then the demon is hatred. He gives men that which is his. He is thus untiring in dividing them, inciting them one against the other. Immediately after falling under his dominion, humanity knew the poison of discord. Adam accuses Eve and vice versa. Cain, overtaken with jealousy, kills his brother Abel. The earth overflowed with violence. Satan works untiringly to divide families through misunderstanding and through mutual lack of acceptance. Divided couples and lost children are the wreckage on which he triumphantly seats himself. He disseminates discord in abundance in communities, the Church, and civil societies. War is his victorious outcry.

Besides the sowing of hatred between men, his other fundamental activity, without a doubt, is seduction. According to Sacred Scripture, it is in this fashion that the demon is most deleterious, reaping his greatest number of victims. It is no coincidence that both the Old Testament and the New Testament begin with the description of those two temptations which marked respectively the fate of misery and the hope of redemption. Jesus warns us many times, saying, "Be vigilant and pray" against the danger we run when the tempter draws near. For this reason, Jesus willed that every time we turn to the Father to offer our petitions, we pray that we are not left to perish in temptation.

What is the profound essence of temptation? It is an instigation toward evil. Because of his hatred of God and his jealousy of man, Satan works in every possible way to dislodge souls from God and from the straight path, seeking to push them into the way of sin and ruin. In order to obtain this result, the shrewd serpent devises true masterpieces of deceit, presenting men with evil disguised as good so that they will desire and choose it. Taking advantage of the human desire for happiness, the tempter presents creatures as the source of man's happiness, in opposition to God and against His will. Satan uses created reality as bait to attract men to himself and to make them his slaves. It is through temptation that Satan obtains his most considerable successes, and it is here that the Christian must fight his most challenging battles.

Temptation Is Universal

Satan tempts every man toward evil, without exception. I remember a conversation with a soul subjected to terrible and continuous temptations. She was distressed and at the point of surrender from one moment to another. This person asked me, "How could it be that with so many men on earth, the devil finds time to occupy himself with me?" This question made me reflect. Certainly, I thought, we cannot attribute to Satan divine omnipotence. However, as a pure spirit, he does have a power and speed of action unknown to us.

Furthermore, who can know the number of the demons of whom Beelzebub is the prince (Matt. 12:24)? Certainly there are many, if we must give the correct interpretation of the biblical image of the red dragon, who, falling to the earth, pulls down a third of the stars of Heaven (Rev. 12:4). The Gospels remind us of a meaningful episode concerning this. Jesus, finding Himself in the region of the Gerasenes, before freeing a possessed man who had been bound with chains on his hands and feet, turns to the demon and asks him his name. He responds, "'Legion,' for many demons had entered him" (Luke 8:30).

There is no doubt that the kingdom of evil is powerful, frightening, and numerous. It is in a position, as experience demonstrates, to cover the entire battlefield and to subject every man to incessant temptation. No soul can delude herself, believing that she can be present as a mere spectator at that spiritual battle in which everyone's eternal destiny is decided. The temptation of the two prototypes of humanity, Adam and Christ, signals the universality of the phenomenon which concerns all men, even those who have been redeemed by the Blood of the Lamb and have entered into the Kingdom of light.

Divine Wisdom did not exclude Jesus or Mary from temptation. God's loving design has decreed that every soul has to face the holy battle, giving to each one all the force and the weapons necessary for winning, so that eternal salvation is both a gift of grace and of our collaborating merit. No one should be fooled into believing that the demon forgets him. Satan, in his incessant activity, desires and seeks out every soul, omitting nothing in his attempt to dominate.

This is why Jesus, dying on the Cross, entrusted, in the person of John, every man to the maternal heart of Mary. Who more than the Virgin, powerful against evil, could defend us from Satan's tremendous snares? God has put the angels under her command so that they will rush to our defense. All skepticism regarding this must disappear before the clear teaching of the Church's Magisterium: "From its beginning until death, human life is surrounded by their watchful care and intercession. 'Beside each believer stands an angel as protector and shepherd leading him to life'" (CCC 336).

Perhaps you think that you are outside of the evil one's grasp because after many victorious battles, you have become stronger in good, and you think that now you have become invulnerable. Beware of this dangerous illusion, dear friend, since Satan and his entire army concentrate their assaults on good and holy souls, judging the tepid and sinners as prey which by now have no chance of escaping. The more a person advances on the spiritual way, the more he is the object of aggression, persecution, and seduction. The evil one is audacious and does not stop in front of anyone. His immense pride has driven him to seduce and to seek to destroy even the Son of God and His work.

This reckless deed, fed by Satan's inextinguishable hatred, has condemned him, but now he pours his ferocity out on the Church and on everything within her that is holy. If the demon leaves you alone, it means that you are in his net. If everything about you is apparently silent, it means that he is weaving his web in silence and darkness. If he openly assaults you, resist him, standing firm in faith, and do not fear him, because the explosion of his fury indicates the failure of his snares. In any case, do not be fooled: he will continue to attempt the capture of your soul until the final instant of your existence on earth.

Temptation Lasts Your Whole Life

There is not a man in the world to whom the devil does not draw near "like a roaring lion, seeking someone to devour" (1 Pet. 5:8). It is licit to wonder if temptation lasts all of our lives without any pause or if there are some welcomed moments of rest. Bear in mind the warning of the Gospel to be constantly on guard and in prayer, because the enemy is hidden and comes as a thief when you least expect it (Matt. 24:43). On the other hand, even if through divine power Satan were forced to retreat in order to return at another moment (Luke 4:13), our human nature, injured by sin and by the world that surrounds us, would be enough to push us daily toward evil.

For this reason, spiritual masters exhort us not to lower our guard for even an instant. Spiritual warfare is a commitment for every day and for every hour. Justly renowned concerning this are the words of the *Imitation of Christ*:

> As long as we live in this world we cannot be without tribulations and temptation. Hence is written in Job: "The life of man upon earth is a temptation" (Job 7:1). Therefore, ought everyone to be on guard against his temptations, and to watch in prayer, lest the devil, who never sleeps, but 'goes about seeking whom he may devour' find room to deceive you. No man is so perfect and holy as not sometimes to have temptations; and we cannot be wholly without them.... There is no Order so holy, nor place so retired, where there are not temptations and adversities.... Many seek to fly from temptations, and fall more grievously into them. By flight alone we cannot win; but by patience and true humility we become stronger than all our enemies. (bk. 1, chap. 13)

It is necessary to bear in mind that although it is the demon who tempts with the purpose of leading us to evil, nevertheless, the power and the Divine Wisdom govern temptation, in the sense that God establishes limits for it; the intensity and the duration are according to the spiritual situation of every soul. Therefore, there is no reason to be amazed that some are strongly perturbed for almost all of the duration of their lives while others endure much lighter temptations. Often after periods of great attacks, there are periods of both peace and serenity. There are situations in which Satan seeks to sift us like wheat (Luke 22:31). In these cases, it is necessary to resist, being strong in the Faith and in prayer.

You do not have to be ashamed of suffering temptations. Even many holy souls, already reaching the summit of perfection, have had to endure humiliating assaults. St. Paul speaks of a thorn in his flesh, of an emissary of Satan sent to harass him. He prayed three times to the Lord that it would be taken away from him, but he received the following response: "My grace is sufficient for you, for my power is made perfect in weakness" (2 Cor. 12:7–9). Even the more humiliating seductions, of which Satan is master, must not discourage you. God permits them so that you do not become puffed up in pride. Face them, humbling yourself and professing your worthlessness.

Some of the greatest saints have been targeted by horrible temptations, even when they were close to death. Do you think that Satan respects you and bows in front of your sanctity? Are you fooled into thinking that he leaves something unattempted in snaring you? The dragon wages war (Rev. 12:17) without exception, leaving you stunned through the ingeniousness and ferocity of his attacks. Woe to us if God does not set limits and does not protect us! You, for your part, must never lose heart and never be discouraged. In temptation, humble your soul under the powerful hand of God, for the Lord saves the humble of spirit and lifts them up.

God Does Not Tempt toward Evil

It should now be clear to you that temptation has as its great director the evil one, whose work is hidden: he seeks to lead you to evil, disguising it as good. For your part, "God cannot be tempted with evil and he himself tempts no one" (James 1:13).

How, then, should we interpret the invocation of the Our Father: "And lead us not into temptation"? The Greek term is difficult to translate, and its full meaning is: "do not allow us to enter into temptation" and "do not let us yield to temptation." With this expression, we thus pray to the celestial Father "not to allow us to take the way that leads to sin" (CCC 2846) but rather to deliver us and keep us from the evil one (John 17:15).

Nevertheless, God does not remove temptation. He permits it. Without divine permission, Satan would not be able to work on earth. The Divine Wisdom has granted the prince of darkness a certain freedom of action, even after he has been dethroned and cast out of this world (John 12:31), permitting him to make war on the Woman and her descendants (Rev. 12:17).

Why does God permit an experience that could lead to our defeat? He permits it to make manifest what dwells deeply in our hearts and to allow the interior man to grow and develop a tried virtue (Rom. 5:3–5). In temptation, it becomes evident who you are and how much you are worth. It is for this reason that grace becomes merit. It is through the struggle that you are confirmed in the good. As a consequence, God permits temptation for a greater good.

From the first centuries of Christianity, the Fathers of the Church had clear ideas concerning this: "God does not want to force any person to do what is good, he wants free human beings.... Temptation has its usefulness. The gifts which our souls have received are unknown to everyone except God. They are unknown even to ourselves. Through temptation they became known. [Temptation] teaches us to know ourselves, in such a way that we discover the fullness of our misery, and it leads us to give thanks for the benefits conferred upon us, that temptation has shown us that we have" (Origen, *De Oratione* 29).

God not only permits but also governs temptation. Satan cannot do whatever he wants, and in any case, he cannot lead us into evil if we do not want to do it. Divine Providence cares with infinite wisdom and goodness for every soul created and redeemed by His infinite love. The when, the where, and the how of every temptation are under the paternal eye of God, who watches so that the evil one does not abuse his power, and He is prompt in granting help to His creatures who call upon His aid. Even though some situations are humanly awful and determined satanic storms seem to stir up everything, you must never lose faith in God.

At times, God permits us to see the horrendous face of evil so that we do not underestimate it. In some cases, He lets the dragon demonstrate all his ferocity so that our eyes are awakened to the horrible dread of Hell, into which we could fall. Satan is underestimated, and so God permits him in temptation to demonstrate all his ferocity in seeking to seduce us and devour us. Nevertheless, we must never forget the exhortation of the apostle Paul: "God is faithful, and he will not let you be tempted beyond your strength, but with the temptation will also provide the way of escape, that you may be able to endure it" (1 Cor. 10:13).

10

The Temptation of Eden

Saints and great spiritual masters have left us, since the first centuries of Christianity, teachings of extraordinary value on the warfare against the demon. Nevertheless, the immutable founts from which we have to draw are the biblical texts, particularly those concerning the two temptations placed at the beginning of the Old and the New Testaments. In those two great events of the history of salvation, God, in His mercy, willed to reveal to us the devious and subtle action of the evil one and to teach us the way to unmask and defeat him. The fall of the first Adam and the victory of Christ are the greatest teachings that humanity has in facing the daily struggle against Satan.

The Serpent in the Earthly Paradise

Beginning with the help of God and of the powerful Virgin to analyze the temptation of Eden (Gen. 3:1–23), I would like first of all to point out to you the presence of Satan in that oasis of divine peace which was the earthly paradise. This fact is already a great teaching which calls each one of us to vigilance and humility. There is no doubt that God conceded a great freedom of action to Satan. There is no place on earth, even though protected, where Satan is not able to be present and to lay his snares. There is no person, no matter how holy, who is immune to Satan's aggressions and his tricks.

Perhaps you are wondering why God provides such a full divine permission. Even though I have reflected many times on this dramatic question, the only response that comes to me is that God completely accepts the risk of having given existence to free creatures. God does not love controlled or conditioned freedom. He desires that our choice for Him arise from the depth of our moral and spiritual self. He concedes to Satan the possibility of leading us along the way of evil so that our choice for good is the consequence of a free and conscious decision. God's justice, however, does not permit the demon to tempt us beyond our strength, so that our ruin, if that unfortunately were to be the outcome of our life, would be attributed exclusively to what we have chosen and willed with full warning and deliberate consent.

Someone could object that if God had not permitted the demon to enter the earthly paradise, humanity would not have known the existential catastrophe into which it has fallen. The loving plan of God would have been implemented without our having to pass through suffering, sin, death, and the danger of eternal perdition. This objection does not realize that God has created free and intelligent beings, such as angels and men, with great risk to Himself. He has created them out of nothing to rejoice in their love; but to have the gift of their love, He had to expose Himself to the possibility of their rejection.

Without the presence of the serpent in the earthly paradise, God would not have been able to sift the heart of man and measure its gratitude and humility in response to the great gifts with which He had totally filled him. God has created the human being with such dignity that we are not able to comprehend it. Adam and Eve enjoyed a special friendship with the Creator in the earthly paradise. They were not servants, but rather they were on close terms with God, who had clothed them with grace, beauty, wisdom, and immortality. Their condition was one of full happiness without any shadows. Their merciful Father had given them good things beyond all limit. What was still missing? Only their gratitude and filial submission, which was something for which the Creator asked in order to admit them to eternal beatitude. But our first parents denied their Father this gratitude; instead of trusting God their benefactor, they gave their confidence to the demon, their enemy and tempter.

The presence of Satan in the earthly paradise is consequently justified by the desire of the Most High to sift the heart of man. However, the serpent crept in, not because God asked him to but because he was moved by his own reasons and desires. What were they? Satan hates God and is envious of man. Jesus says of Satan that he is a liar and murderer (John 8:44). In order to complete the picture, we will have to add that he is also a thief (John 10:1). He wanted to steal the gifts man had received, first the grace, and then the condition of happiness in which he had been placed. Naturally, his final goal is to steal your soul, depriving you of the eternal beatitude.

Remember, dear friend, that when you are in friendship with God and have received some particular gifts, Satan will not remain quiet until he has denuded you of everything. He offers you what is his in order to rob you of what is God's. He gives you fool's gold to deprive you of true gold. In following him, you will always find yourself in the end fighting the swine for husks. When you receive a grace, Satan does not remain passive but immediately begins to work to steal it (Luke 8:12). If he is unsuccessful, he does everything he can to keep you from seeing that grace so that you cannot give thanks and bring it to fruition. Be vigilant, because being clothed with sanctifying grace and having the benefit of receiving special gifts does not exempt you from temptation but exposes you to greater assaults, which you will be able to reject with that humble prayer and confidence Adam and Eve lacked.

The Serpent Was the Shrewdest of All the Beasts

Satan is shrewd. What is this shrewdness of which the biblical author speaks? It is the art of deceiving. In this, Satan is the master. Lies and violence are the fundamental characteristics of his proud self (John 8:44). No one can compete with the demon's shrewdness. Anyone foolish enough to listen to the demon will become enmeshed. Jesus emphasizes that Satan is the "father of lies." Consider that Adam and Eve had, among the other gifts, divine wisdom. Nevertheless, the evil one succeeded in seducing them.

Are you fooled into thinking that you are able to escape Satan's tricks? This was possible only for Jesus and Mary. It is only through prayer and God's assistance that the saints are able to escape and evade the evil one's traps. It is incredible how many people the great deceiver succeeds in deceiving, even among those who, like Adam and Eve, are clothed with sanctifying grace. The saints were so diffident that even when they were granted extraordinary graces, they preferred to place everything under the judgment of their confessor.

The authority of the Church is indeed the great remedy that God has put in opposition to the almost limitless capacity of the demon to deceive. Think of all the errors that, even in the sphere of churchmen, have been proliferated throughout the course of history, be it concerning the truths of the Faith or morals. Consider how many men, even scholars and well-educated people, have been dragged along the way of error by the great deceiver.

Satan's success consists in presenting what is false as if it were truth. If you were pure of heart, as were Jesus and Mary, you would immediately recognize the lie, but you are not pure of heart. Satan studies the hidden hungers of your person and presents you the truth, not as it is in itself, but as you would like it to be. Today, for example, because people do not want to cease sinning, he convinces them that Hell is empty. Infinite are the errors he provides for our turbid desires. Men are fed with and believe in falsehood because it agrees with their carnal selves. Satan fools them into believing that they are in truth, when in reality, they are blinded. Woe to the one who says that he sees, not knowing that he has been blinded by the enemy (John 9:41)!

Satan Turns to Eve

Satan gives the first demonstration of his inimitable shrewdness in deciding to turn to the woman. If he had decided to speak with both of our first parents, it would have been much more difficult to deceive them together. A united couple with good understanding between themselves would have constituted a much greater obstacle. If Satan had conquered Adam first, it would have been much more difficult to convince Eve to disobey the commandment of God. Woman needs man for protection, but in sensing the complexity of a situation and making the appropriate decisions, it is she who is the protagonist.

Satan knows the influence of woman on man, more so than man is willing to admit to himself. The evil one is aware of that, and he knows that if he succeeds in conquering Eve, Adam too will quickly fall into his hands. Indeed, having tasted the fruit, she offered it to her husband, who ate it without any discussion.

One of the better cards played by the infernal serpent is that of using woman for his aims and making her his ally. It is a subtle strategy that guarantees him great success. God confronts Satan on this fundamental point, putting in opposition to him the Virgin Mary and, with her, all those great women saints who marked the navigation of the Church through the centuries. God-fearing women are a great strength for families and the Church. Satan rarely succeeds in insinuating himself into families where the wives are faithful or into ecclesiastical communities where in the heart of the virgins burns the pure love of God. But if women do not do their duty, who will ever be able to assess the ruin for families and for the Church?

Consider further how the very shrewd serpent succeeds with great cleverness in seducing the people who are close to you, without your even noticing it. Often, not succeeding in harming you directly, he insinuates himself into whoever is closest to you and bound to you by bonds of affection. This could happen with spouses, children, friends, associates, or coworkers. Having obtained their defection, he seeks to hurt and possibly seduce you. Understand how vigilant you must be in all of your responsibilities so that the enemy does not succeed in introducing and provoking irreparable damage.

The First Lie

Satan begins with a lie so well conjured that it almost seems true. He has an unmistakable style. God had said to man that he could eat of all the trees in the Garden, but not of the tree of the knowledge of good and evil, because eating of it would result in his death (Gen. 2:16–17). The great deceiver shrewdly changed the commandment of God. In the form of a question, not to reveal himself too much, he asked Eve: "Did God say, 'You shall not eat of any tree of the garden?'" (Gen. 3:1).

The mere fact that the serpent changed what the Lord had said in the clear simplicity of His Word must always make you suspicious. It is the typical tactic of the false prophets, among whom Satan is both the first and the master. Furthermore, the adulteration of the Word of the Creator is subtly turned to darken the image. It is a clever insinuation that presents God as the One who prevents you from enjoying life and the beauty of creation. Satan always seeks to harm the image of God that He Himself has luminously revealed to your mind and heart. Satan slanders God, defames Him, and presents Him in a distorted way. He achieves this goal by presenting to you, in a distorted form, the truth which God has revealed to us and which the Church presents to us to be believed.

Understand, dear friend, that Satan always aims for the essential because his main concern is to harm your faith. Through teachers of error, particularly the mass media whom he deftly controls under his influence, and by making full use also of prejudices, errors, and the infected hearts of those with whom you associate daily, Satan aims to undermine your confidence in God and your adherence to the light of truth. Once he has overrun the stronghold of your faith, he is easily in a position to take control of your entire household.

Eve Did Not Have to Respond

The gravest error Eve could have committed was that of responding to the evil one. When you feel the hissing of the serpent, you must not choose to look at him and even less pause to listen to the lies he proposes to you. When temptation presents itself to your heart under the form of a thought, an image, or a proposal, you must immediately avert the eyes of your heart and turn them to God in prayer. If you halt even for a moment to regard what Satan proposes to you, he attracts you into his sphere, and your defeat is secure.

Eve should not have waited even for the serpent to finish speaking, but as soon as she heard the voice of the liar, she should have plugged her ears to hear no more. Temptation should be rejected from the beginning; we must remove our hearts from the tempter and turn them toward God. This readiness is the fruit of a pure interior disposition and of an assiduous exercise in mortification, but that is what saves us. If man accepts "entering into temptation," it is going to be very difficult for him to defeat it. This is the reason that great spiritual masters teach unanimously that the fire of temptation must be smothered immediately upon its birth, before it becomes a devastating conflagration.

In consenting to listen to the voice of the liar, in reality, Eve had already opened a small crack, into which the venomous serpent immediately crept to deal the fatal bite. Responding to the serpent, with the apparent motivation of correcting his lie, the woman referred to God's command, reducing its efficacy. God had said that if they ate of the tree, they would die. She responded by removing the certainty, having already begun to evaluate in her heart, at least, the distant possibility that the punishment was not certain. When temptation rages and in your heart you begin to minimize the consequences of sin, it means that the serpent is already squeezing you in his coils. When you ask, "What evil is there?" the moment of surrender has arrived and you are already at his mercy.

The Second Lie

You have already yielded to temptation when you begin to take into consideration what Satan proposes to you, even if you hold it to be false. In reality, the wily tempter always offers you something that strongly attracts you in the core of your being. You cannot listen to his lie without making a great effort in your heart to reject it. He presents God's command as a limit to your freedom and as a mortification of your desires. If you do not immediately make the effort to reject Satan's allurements, you will be overwhelmed by everything in you which has not yet been made subject to God.

Although Eve sought to contradict Satan with her tongue, she had already conceded in her heart. She behaved like a woman who flees in the hope that the hunter will capture her as soon as possible. You do the same when you tell yourself that you do not want to sin, while in your heart, evil has already crept in. You are calculating its consequences. Perhaps it is not true that evil causes so much damage, you say, reassuring yourself. But a breach has been opened in your defenses, and the serpent has eagerly crept in. His bite is sudden, precise, mortal: "Certainly you will not die," he hisses. He has the arrogance typical of false teachers who trumpet their errors as if they were indisputable dogmas with no need of proof. As an example, ask anyone who claims that Hell does not exist, or that if it does, it is empty, on which biblical text the claim is based.

Satan tells you exactly what you want to hear, once you have entered into temptation. He persuades you that God's sanction on sin is an inconsistent menace: "You certainly will not die," he said to our first parents. "You will not go to Hell," he says today. "It is not true that evil causes evil; it is not true that the way of sin leads to ruin and perdition. The contrary is true!" he hisses in your ears. You listen to him because you now see with his eyes, and your confidence in the truth of God is itself almost completely eradicated from your heart.

The Third Lie

Now you have been persuaded into thinking that God lies and Satan tells the truth, a drastic affirmation that you would have never confessed. Next you affirm that the commandments of God are an invention of priests and of a Church no longer moving with the times. Look around and see the immense herd of evil. "Everyone does this; why should I comport myself differently?" you repeat many times, attempting to convince and calm yourself.

God said to our first parents: "In the day that you eat of it, you shall die." Satan once affirmed in a convincing tone: "You certainly will not die." God says to you through the teaching of the Church and through the voice of your conscience that the way of sin leads to ruin. You do not believe Him, but you put your faith in the liar who, finding no resistance in your heart, now has the courage to accuse God of lying and of jealousy against man. Hissing with a truly luciferian arrogance, Satan scoffs, "God knows that when you eat of it your eyes will be opened, and you will be like God, knowing good and evil" (Gen. 3:5).

Satan, having found favorable terrain, sows his poison in full measure. He presents God, your creator and benefactor, as the adversary of your happiness. The Divine Word taught you that the commandments are "light for the eyes and joy for the heart," and their fulfillment makes man grow and renders him happy. The liar, having destroyed your trust in God and in His true Word, thrusts toward his final aim, that of bringing you to open rebellion against God.

Here the ancient serpent injects into your heart that which is his. First, he offers you the goods of the world, which arouse human passions. Sex, money, pleasure, pride, and power are the bait with which he captures innumerable souls, but his final goal is to bring them to disobey, rebel, and deny God. Through sin, Satan wants to steal you from God and make you a slave in his dark kingdom. You believe him because he arouses the hidden desires of your being. The consequence for you is death. Dear friend, God does not lie. Whoever eats what Satan offers experiences the most terrible of deaths, in which the soul becomes like an arid desert, inhabited only by serpents and scorpions.

The Seduction

Now the shrewd deceiver has completed his work and can remain quiet, waiting for the fruits of his labor. Now the great seduction is consummated in your mind. Satan has drawn near with a thought, seeking to attract your attention to him. It was a hissing lie, but you have not made the effort in your heart to reject him and turn your eyes in prayer to God, your Lord, professing your unworthiness, asking for His grace, declaring your obedience and filial faithfulness. Only with this effort of the soul, which should be made at the beginning of temptation, would you be able to succeed and obtain the victory.

Finding the door open, Satan has entered and persuaded you that the way of evil does not lead to death but rather to the realization of happiness. What were Adam and Eve lacking in the earthly paradise? They were able to taste all the beauty and grandeur of life in humble submission and dedication to God. What is lacking in the life of a man who lives with confidence in his celestial Father who abundantly gives both material and spiritual goods to His children?

Satan presents you with a vision of life in which you are the only master and therefore can do whatever you want; a life without God, submission, obedience, and commandments; a life in which you are your own god. You, like Eve, are hypnotized by the music of the serpent and, spellbound, you gaze at the tree of the knowledge of good and evil. Now Satan has persuaded you that life without God, without rules and responsibilities, in which you can do whatever you want, deciding as you like what is good and what is evil, is beautiful and full of fascination. "The woman saw that the tree was good for food, and that it was a delight to the eyes, and that the tree was to be desired to make one wise" (Gen. 3:6).

The summit of temptation is represented by the false beauty of evil. Is evil beautiful? Nothing could be more false. Satan has taken possession of you and deceived you into believing that joy and happiness are brought to you. His beauty is bait that attracts in order to capture. Behind the false light of an immoral life is hidden the sarcastic smile of the dark one. Evil promises but does not fulfill. Disillusion always follows illusion. Regrettably, man never ceases deluding himself. Why? It is because of the unlimited ability of the deceiver, who can persuade you every time you listen to him, even though you have already been deceived by him innumerable times. Presenting you an evil as if it were a good is the supreme art of the tempter. Here is the crux of his lie which you are always ready to believe.

Eve deceived herself that she would be acquiring "wisdom" in taking the way of evil. The followers of the evil one are always very proud. They represent culture, science, and knowledge. They feel themselves superior to the "fanatics" who base life on the catechism and on what is taught by the priests. Theirs is the knowledge of the blind. They do not know where they come from, who they are, or where they are going. They also do not know what their lives are about, and like berserk mosquitoes, they are cast onto false lights that burn them. How much higher and more useful is the wisdom of the simple!

The Decision

Now temptation has taken root in your heart. The unrepressed desire has grown enormously and has conquered you. You want with all your strength to have whatever Satan has proposed to you. Nothing could stop you. Do not people kill for passion, for a position of power, for ambition, or for a little bit of money? Like a drug addict in need of a fix, you seek to grab the fruit of the tree. Temptation has become a fever that devours you. The burning thirst of evil has penetrated your veins. Now Satan possesses your heart and leads you as he led Judas. The devil first slipped the thought of betrayal into the heart of the apostle (John 13:2), then, when the conquering of his heart was complete, he took over his person (John 13:27).

It is the moment of the decision. Eve "took of its fruit and ate" (Gen. 3:6). The conclusive moment of temptation is the decision of the will. Satan works on your intellect, presenting evil disguised as good, but it is you who must give consent: first internally, accepting what the tempter offers you and handing over to him the key to your heart; then the act becomes exterior, and you complete the wicked deed.

Eve first looked at and desired the fruit of the tree, then she took it, and finally she ate it. So you first caress temptation with your eyes, then you decide to consent, and finally you bring the act to completion. The moment of sin coincides with your consent, even if only internally (Matt. 5:28). The exterior act completes and aggravates the evil committed. Satan seduces, but you are the one who decides. Even though his seduction is very powerful, he cannot bend your will to do evil. Even though the tempest of thoughts, desires, resentment, and hatred he stirs in your heart is overwhelming, there is no sin without your free and conscious consent. Eve sinned because she wanted to sin. God has put our will exclusively in our hands.

The Corruption

There are apostles of evil. They are people who, besides ruining themselves, drag along other souls also. They have perverted themselves into becoming demons, as St. Catherine of Siena asserted, and thus "fulfill the office of the demons," inducing others to sin. It is truly said that one never sins alone. Our sin is negatively reflected in our neighbors. If we do not repent quickly and return to God, the heart is hardened, and, almost to reassure ourselves, we drag others along the way of ruin.

Eve was so possessed by evil that she did not hesitate to entice Adam also. "She also gave some to her husband, and he ate" (Gen. 3:6). When you examine your life, remember all the times that by your words, evil example, and complicity, you have pushed your neighbor into the arms of the evil one. Think of all those souls that are lost in sin because of you. Repent before God, repair the damages you have caused, and make yourself an apostle of good.

The corruptors of souls are the great strength of the demon. In the contemporary world, they occupy very significant and visible positions in various fields such as sociology, science, politics, and economics, including within the realm of the mass media. They have learned the vernacular of flattery and lies from their teacher. Despising truth and exalting error, they disparage good and virtue while exalting evil and vice. They are the faithful servants of Satan, and they will go with him to his kingdom of death in recompense.

Watch out for such people, even if they are very close to you and united to you by bonds of affection. You show your worthiness as a human being by saying no to evil, even if the one who proposes it is most dear to you. If Adam had said no to Eve, he would have undoubtedly saved himself and perhaps even her. No human respect, no bond of friendship, no reason of human nature, nor any interest must ever cause you stay with anyone who proposes evil. It is much better to lose a friend or family member than to lose God for all of eternity.

Nevertheless, Adam took the fruit Eve offered him without argument, and he ate it. He blindly followed his wife, even when she fell into the abyss. How many behave like this! Like leaves in the wind, they are dragged where the world wants, and Satan rejoices over the spoils obtained so cheaply. The law of the herd, public opinion polls, and social brainwashing dominate the modern world. You, however, must be very attentive to the voice of God. Keep your conscience illuminated by the Church and never stray from her, no matter what others think, even if they are those whom you love the most.

From Disillusionment to Illusion

When man commits evil, he is inevitably degraded. He then opens his eyes, and all that before seemed beautiful and desirable now entirely loses its attractiveness. First evil attracts you, then it poisons you. From the illusion of obtaining much happiness follows both disillusionment and disappointment. Once the fruit was eaten, "the eyes of both were opened" (Gen. 3:7). Adam and Eve had deluded themselves into thinking that they could become "like God," but they found themselves deprived of divinity and its gifts. The conscience begins to feel remorse. But that God whom you have driven from your heart by sinning does not abandon you. In His goodness, He makes you hear His voice in the depths of your being. It is a voice that disapproves of the evil you have committed and, at the same time, is an invitation to return to the straight way.

Consider this great grace that opens the eyes after the satanic temptation. It is the moment in which, if you are honest with yourself, you realize that Satan has deceived you. With all that he has offered you, he has succeeded in destroying your dignity, morality, and your soul. He has given you something, but he himself has taken your heart. You, like Adam and Eve, realize your nakedness. You have been stripped of sanctifying grace and of the gifts of spiritual beauty and wisdom that adorned you: now you see yourself in your misery.

The disillusionment that comes after every sin, with the verification of the deception, the remorse of conscience, and the consciousness of the damages you have suffered, constitutes a moment of great grace, even though in the context of a spiritual catastrophe. After every sin, the Divine Wisdom opens our eyes so that we see the despicable face of evil. This always happens unless a person, persevering on the way of ruin, suffocates his conscience and hardens his heart.

Adam and Eve, having realized the lie of the tempter and the existential catastrophe into which they had fallen, would have been able and should have cried out to God from the depths of their misery. The Creator in His goodness would have listened to them and would have come to their aid. So we, dear friend, have at the moment of the grace of disillusionment the possibility of a ready rehabilitation, if we turn humbly and contritely to that God whom we have foolishly abandoned.

Unfortunately, this happens all too rarely. More often, man falls again into that satanic deception, desiring to try again the fruit which has proven to be so untrustworthy and poisonous. The disillusionment is followed by a new illusion, and this process continues so that man enters into a deadly mechanism that crushes the soul, driving it to blindness and to total death.

Many men waste their lives following illusions which are followed immediately by disillusionment. "Every one who drinks of this water will thirst again," declares Jesus (John 4:13). Only the mercy of God can break this satanic chain which renders us slaves, but you must cooperate with the grace which opens your eyes every time you do evil. Think of the last sin you committed. Were you happy to place your trust in the demon? Didn't you become disillusioned, saddened, and degraded? Why, then, do you wish to repeat the same experience, believing again and again the allurements of the tempter?

There may come a time in which, having sinned, your eyes are no longer opened. It is a very alarming signal, because it means you are entering the spiritual status of impenitence. This happens when you advance unperturbed along the way of perversion and your conscience is finally snuffed out completely. Then the worst crimes can be committed without your feeling remorse. How many souls move in this level of deep darkness, in which they have given their unconditional consent to Satan and to his kingdom of perdition! Only a great grace, such as Judas had with the reawakening of conscience, could now save them.

The Fig Leaves

The term "fig leaf" is a popular idiomatic expression. The sign that in our times men have returned to the perversion of our first parents is demonstrated by the fact that now even the fig leaves are considered superfluous. It is a terrible sign of corruption, because it means that our generation is no longer ashamed of evil, but flaunts and exalts it. Now our times have reached the final stage of depravation, when sin comes out from the darkness of shame in which the light was confining it and exhibits its arrogant and wicked face to the world. Today, evil openly challenges God, almost to the point of provoking His justice.

When humanity touches those abysses of iniquity, it will mean that the end times have arrived, in which will be revealed "the man of lawlessness" and "the son of perdition" (2 Thess. 2:3), as St. Paul called the antichrist. Before arriving at this final stage of moral degradation, man, who is naturally oriented to good, feels shame for the evil committed and seeks to cover it. The fig leaves woven together by Adam and Eve indicate the uneasiness which every man and certainly you, too, experience after every evil act.

One feels dirty after sinning. If you were in God's grace beforehand, you now experience all the anguish of lost innocence. Even if you are already moving along the way of perdition, you realize that the evil you commit hangs over you like a great weight and crushes the last vestiges of your self-esteem. You need to hide and cover yourself with a varnish of respectability. You need to appear presentable to yourself and to others. Not having the good will to change internally, you construct a mask that allows you to appear differently from the way you really are. You have enrolled yourself in the undying confraternity of the Pharisees of all times.

Once you have accepted the tempter's flatteries, you have only two possibilities before you. The first and only valid choice is to repent, which allows you, by the absolution of a priest, to regain the innocence lost. This is a difficult way, and it demands the heart's effort to detach oneself from evil. Few are those who take this road. The other possibility is to hide from yourself and from others the evil committed and to construct a façade of goodness. Jesus branded the people who behaved like this with fire, calling them "whitewashed tombs" (Matt. 23:27). This way is apparently more comfortable, but have you considered where it leads?

Remorse of Conscience

The way of evil leads to eternal perdition. For that reason, God sends His grace so that the sinner would not perish but rather would be converted and live. But you, instead of repenting of the evil committed, have just covered it. Playing the role of the honest person for yourself and others, you deceive yourself that the game is over. Do you think that God has not seen you, or that He did not notice, or that He is not interested in your conduct? You are mistaken, because God is a Father who takes maximum care of every one of His children and does not let them perish in the jaws of the lion.

Before they had finished braiding the modest fig leaves with their skillful craftsmanship, Adam and Eve "heard the sound of the Lord God walking in the garden in the cool of the day" (Gen. 3:8). The poor deluded couple believed they had eradicated God simply by taking His place and determining by themselves what was right and what was wrong. However, God continues to exist even if we deny Him. Even if you obstinately affirm that there is no sun, it does not cease to shine in the immensity of the celestial sphere.

This biblical passage reminds me of an experience I had as a boy. A group of friends and I were climbing into some cherry trees that were full of beautiful and tasty fruit, so attractive in those hard years for the poor after World War II. Suddenly, I saw the owner of the trees approaching, who I thought had not seen me. I held my breath in the hope that I would remain unobserved. The farmer laid the ladder against the trunk of the tree and began to ascend with a big stick in his hand. It seemed that he wanted to hook some of the cherries that were far away, but in reality, I was the target. With one leap, I jumped down from the tree and ran away.

Dear friend, do not be deceived in thinking that this world does not have an owner. If you eat from the forbidden tree, be assured that He will make you feel it. You think that you are scot-free, but in the depths of your soul, not yet hardened by evil, you feel Him approaching. Even after you have sinned, God makes you feel His existence and presence. It is an incommensurable grace. Do you not sense, after every fall, the voice of conscience reproving you and calling you to feel remorse?

You would like God to leave you alone, but He does not give you a break. His voice follows you everywhere. The remorse of conscience is the greatest torment of the sinner. As St. Catherine of Siena states, it is like a dog that barks to warn of the danger to the soul. Others compare it to a worm that does not leave you alone, continually gnawing on your insides. There is no peace for the sinner. In his sleepless nights, he feels God coming and going before the door of his heart. What does your heart prompt you to do? Will you confront your sin with the audacity of one who believes in his forgiveness, or will you fall ever deeper into the abyss, further and further away from God?

Death by Suffocation

You have had the grace of disillusionment that has shown you the deceptive face of the evil one. Yet not even this is enough to bring you to repentance. Now the Divine Mercy concedes to you another grace, that is, the remorse of conscience. It is the voice of God that disapproves of the evil done, pronouncing a judgment to which you cannot raise any objections. The light of reason would like you to change your direction and return to the good road, leaving that way of apparent ease that is, in reality, always more destructive. Yet you are determined to continue, as if the evil had enchanted you. When the serpent injects his venom and you have allowed it to spread throughout your body, it is not easy to detoxify yourself. Sin has an intoxication that conquers and enchants.

So what do you do? Instead of responding to the divine admonition of conscience, you seek first to quiet it and then to suffocate it. You too, like our first parents, flee from the presence of the Lord God, who questions you about what you have done, and you hide yourself in the middle of the trees of the garden. The suffocation of your own conscience is one of the gravest crimes man can commit. It occurs little by little, gradually suppressing all remorse. When the voice of God is silent within us, our spiritual death is complete, and the soul is possessed by Satan. Only a great miracle of grace, like the one Judas had (Matt. 27:3), could again reawaken it.

You have entered into that tremendous valley of sin where every light is snuffed out. God passes by, and you hide yourself so as not to be discovered. You do not want to see or hear Him. You have closed the doors and windows so that not even a single ray of the sun filters through. You have burnt bridges with all good people and can no longer support their presence. Everything that reminds you of God and the straight path now bothers you. Now you are interested only in the company of the wicked, who approve of your conduct and justify it along with theirs. Enclosed in your own darkness, you hide yourself from God in the hope that you will be left to enjoy the trees of the garden without any further disturbance.

The Call to Conversion

Will God let His beloved children perish in the lion's jaws? Even though our responsibility for traveling along the evil way is great, God has a fatherly heart that tries every possible means to save His children. Do you remember the parable of the lost sheep? In a certain sense, it is even more touching than the parable of the prodigal son. Here, the Divine Mercy is not bound to wait for the face of His child looming on the horizon but rather immediately takes the initiative, going out to search for His child and allowing Himself no rest until he is found.

The Lord God also went on a search for Adam, who had fled into the darkness of evil and was deaf to every interior admonition. Not seeing him, God called him with a voice so strong that Adam could not avoid hearing it: "Where are you?" asked the Omnipotent One, who knew well where the child to whom He had given so many gifts had hidden himself. There is no place in the world in which one can hide himself from God. "If I ascend to heaven, thou art there; if I make my bed in Sheol, thou art there!" exclaims the Psalmist (Psalm 139:8). It is useless for men to attempt to build a world without God. Not even a hair from one's head can claim independence from Him (Matt. 5:36, 37). The presence of God surrounds the world to save it, not to suffocate it as Satan does.

The trumpet of salvation sounds and will continue to sound everywhere in the world until the end of time. That powerful cry, "Adam, where are you?" runs through human history, from its beginning until its completion. God does not abandon the callous sinner, even one who obstinately pursues the way of evil. He never ceases to call the sinner to repentance at crucial moments. Until the last instant of life, God throws a lifeline to save the sinner from being swallowed by the infernal whirlpool. No man will ever be able to accuse the Merciful One of not having called him strongly enough to be heard. If a soul falls into eternal perdition, it will not be because of a defect of grace; it is exclusively the soul's own fault.

The Terror of the Impenitent Sinner

Our first parents enjoyed the very sweet friendship of God before sin. After Satan pushed them into disobedience, they dared not face Him, but they hid themselves because of their fear. I do not need to explain to you what it means to be afraid of God, since no man is free from this. It is the consequence of the evil in us. If we have difficulties experiencing God as our Father and having confidence in His infinite love, it is because we do not behave as His children. If we have not been loyal to a person, we do not dare look him in the face. The more a man sins, the more he flees from the presence of God and seeks refuge in the darkness. Victory over fear coincides with the acquisition of innocence.

Adam was afraid because of the sin he committed, but the more one advances along the way of evil, the more fear is transformed into terror. Many deny that God exists, but in reality, they are afraid of His judgment. The nights of sinners are sleepless. The anguish over their present situation and the future outcome of their lives does not allow them a moment of rest. Sin does not bear sanctity. When Jesus advances, the demons retreat; they come out into the open and flee. Have you noticed how impenitent sinners are very uncomfortable in sacred places or when they are close to people in whom they notice God's presence?

Fear generates aggressiveness, which often becomes wickedness. How else would you explain the continuing persecutions of good people in every period of history? Satan, the first sinner, cannot bear the holiness of God and combats it with all of his might. The book of Revelation represents well this ferocity with the image of the dragon who first seeks to devour the baby just born and then to hurl himself against the woman who gave birth. The obstinate sinner sooner or later becomes a persecutor, because evil cannot bear the good and seeks to wipe it from the face of the earth.

Judgment and Punishment

If you repent, God absolves you. If you do not repent, you must face judgment. If Adam, instead of hiding himself, had gone to meet the Lord God, invoking divine mercy and pardon, the sin would have been removed and his honor as a child reintegrated. Sins presented to the Divine Mercy in the sacrament of Confession are absolved and no longer remembered. If the impious "turns from his sin and does what is lawful and right ... none of the sins that he has committed shall be remembered" (Ezek. 33:14–16). Consider how important it is to ask forgiveness from God while the necessary time is granted to us. Judgment will come at the moment of death, when every sin committed will be placed before us as a reason for condemnation.

The judgment of a penitent sinner concludes with an embrace. Remember the words Jesus addressed to the thief who was on His right and who was asking Him to remember him when He would enter into His kingdom: "Truly, I say to you, today you will be with me in Paradise" (Luke 23:43). On the contrary, the judgment of the impenitent sinner manifests in the light of God all the sins he has committed and for which he has never demonstrated any sorrow. Uselessly will you seek to pass your responsibilities onto others, just as Adam and Eve did. God knows our hearts in a way that we ourselves do not even know them. He knows the responsibilities of everyone, and any attempt to blame others would be futile.

"The woman whom thou gavest to be with me, she gave me fruit of the tree, and I ate" (Gen. 3:12). Notice that our first parents were not really penitent. Adam subtly accused God for his fall, because it was God who put by his side the woman temptress. Eve, for her part, sought to excuse herself, accusing the serpent of having deceived her. In reality, each of us must answer for our own actions. Others can push you toward evil, but if you do not want it, all of their efforts will be in vain. Sin is always desired by the one who commits it. If that is not the case, there is no sin. Others have enticed you, but it is you who have eaten the forbidden fruit.

Yet the irreparable tragedy does not consist in having committed evil but in not having repented of it. It is the absence of contrition that condemns man. This, at its roots, is the sin against the Holy Spirit. God knows that even after the Redemption, men have continued to sin. If we look around us, do we not see the earth flooded by a muddy ocean unlike anything that has occurred in the past? It is for this reason that Jesus commanded His apostles and His Church to preach throughout the whole world, until the conclusion of history, repentance and the forgiveness of sins (Luke 24:47). Only the decision to change his life preserves man from the judgment of condemnation.

In the end, dear friend, evil is punished. There is either repentance or punishment. Nobody can think that he must answer only to himself for his life. Satan deceived you by presenting an absolute freedom to choose between good and evil without any reference to the law of God and to the voice of your conscience. When the games are finished and the time of forgiveness has expired, you will realize that you must answer to your Creator for every instant of your existence.

Death without the invocation of forgiveness is Satan's greatest victory. Every other one of his deceptions can be corrected by returning to God with humility and a contrite heart. The ultimate strategy of the evil one is to bring you before the Divine Judge with an obstinate and impenitent heart.

11

The Temptation of Jesus in the Desert

From Eden to the Desert

In my opinion, it is a fact of great importance that both the Old and the New Testaments begin with a story of temptation, the effects of which have been decisive in the history of salvation. This means that temptation is a fundamental spiritual experience, on which depends the outcome of every man's life. The protagonists are not marginal figures but the old and the New Adam, who are the prototypes of humanity in its history of perdition and salvation.

We can say that the two fundamental phases of human history are derived from these two temptations. From the first, which caused a spiritual and existential catastrophe, began to flow the river of evil, which has flooded the world and still threatens to sweep it away. From the second has gushed forth the living and sanctifying water of good that flows on the arid and parched earth of souls, giving them renewed life, strength, and support for the holy battle.

They are two temptations with radically different outcomes. In the first temptation, man is defeated, and Satan is the victor. Created with great dignity in the image of God and clothed with the divine gifts of grace, man, in falling for the temptation, lost everything and began a life of darkness, suffering, slavery to evil, and death. We all find ourselves subject to temptation, because no one, except the Son of God and the Most Holy Virgin, passes totally unharmed through the snares set by the ancient adversary in his shrewdness and malice.

Because of Adam's defeat, humanity has fallen under the dictatorship of evil and, even though man's free will sustains the possibility of resisting the tempter, evil has flooded the earth. Thus, the apostle John was able to affirm that the entire world has been placed under the power of the evil one (1 John 5:19). All our experiences of defeat only reproduce and actualize that defeat of our first parents, prolonging in us its consequences. In those immortal pages of Genesis, we discover our daily drama as creatures unfaithful to God, vacillating in our faith when the tempter plays his seductive music and ever ready to throw away the precious pearls of grace in exchange for a sparkling piece of glass.

In the second temptation, which has Jesus in the desert as the protagonist (Matt. 4:1–11), Satan is defeated. It is a defeat so clear, indisputable, and peremptory that it alarms the tempter. He realizes with panic, rage, and ferocity that the moment has arrived in which he will be driven away from souls, losing his maleficent power over them. The devil knew that he had the promised Messiah before him, but his immense pride deceived him into thinking he would be able to defeat Him. Exiting humiliated from the greatest duel that ever took place between good and evil, the great dragon later returned and lashed out with all the dark power of Hell in the days of the Passion, when God made use of Satan's own plan of destruction and death to defeat him.

In the temptation of the desert, humanity finds its long-awaited redemption. The New Adam did not overcome evil merely for Himself but for all of us. His victory already contains the seed of victory for us all; now, in Jesus and with Jesus, every Christian can face the evil one and defeat him. Meditating on the temptations of Jesus in the desert is fundamental to the spiritual life. They have been at the center of the spiritual meditations of innumerable souls. There is no better source of efficacious teaching to discover the tremendous snares of the tempter and to victoriously reject them. If in retracing the vicissitudes of Eden, we have understood how man proceeded toward his ruin, now, by meditating on the epic struggle in the desert, we can learn what weapons to use as we proceed on the way of good and of salvation.

A Man Is Not Enough to Defeat Satan

Before entering into the biblical text, I would like to make an introductory consideration. If it is an error to amplify the strength of Satan by considering him to be practically invincible, it would also be profoundly erroneous to underestimate his strength. We have not even the faintest idea of the evil one's power of deception and destruction. If Divine Omnipotence had not limited Satan, bending him to the divine designs, he would have already transformed all of God's creation into his infernal kingdom of death.

One of the limits God has put on the action of Satan is the will of man. Satan's power to seduce can be exercised on the mind but not on the will. If man does not want, he does not sin. This consideration remains a key point regarding spiritual warfare. Only God is able to efficaciously influence human will, orienting it toward good but always respecting its freedom. Satan can urge the will, but he cannot bend it to evil.

We do not recognize the power of Satan merely by his successes but also and especially by the fact that God had to face him personally in order to defeat him. Man would not have been enough, not even one with such an extraordinary character as St. John the Baptist, the greatest man born of woman (Matt. 11:11). Even the Virgin Mary drew all of her strength, by which she rejected the serpent, from the grace of Christ with which she was completely filled. The fact remains that God did not send a man to face the evil one, but He Himself came down to earth. The Incarnate Word, that is, God made man, is the great warrior who struggled throughout His life to acquire the victory.

Do not, therefore, be deceived into believing that you can face Satan with your strength alone. You would be dragged away in an instant like a leaf in the wind. The presumption with which, on some occasions, ascetics and exorcists have faced him has cost them dearly. Men abandoned to themselves before the slimy serpent are like spellbound frogs that he swallows as he desires. It is with the awareness of your nothingness and by remaining well-rooted in the victory of Jesus that you will be able to resist and win. You will not achieve the victory, but the grace of Christ in you, which works marvels in every heart that is humble and pure, will triumph.

Satan Launches the Challenge

The temptation of Jesus at the beginning of His public life was foreseen in the divine plan for salvation. The evangelists unanimously emphasize that it was the Spirit who led Jesus into the desert to be tempted by the devil (Matt. 4:1, Mark 1:12, Luke 4:1). It is that same Spirit who a little earlier had descended on Jesus in the form of a dove, filling Jesus with Himself. The Divine Wisdom established that the New Adam, the prototype of the new humanity, would begin His mission with the most shining victory in order to confirm that the time of redemption had now arrived.

The scent of holiness emanating from the one who was Full of Grace and from her virginally-generated Son was not lost on Satan, who was perfectly aware that the divine plan foreseen from all eternity was beginning to be set in motion. As in the Garden of Eden, he came readily to the appointment. Satan knew that he was in the presence of the Son of God, and it was not by chance that his temptations were aimed at harming the divine identity of Jesus or his mission as the Savior.

Perhaps you are amazed that the seducer dared to tempt the One he knew to be the Son of the Most High. His pride, dear friend, is so immeasurable that it prevents him from being aware of his own limits, while his hatred is so strong and violent that it drives him to interfere with the divine plans of salvation in every way and at any cost. Has the prince of this world hesitated to conceive of a plan for eliminating the Incarnate Word? Satan is aware of his own great strength and challenges the Omnipotent in the conquest for souls, seeking to destroy all of His projects of mercy. There is nothing God starts that Satan does not immediately rush to impede. It is no mistake that the word *devil*, from the Greek *diabolos*, means "the one who divides."

The tempter does not fear God and boldly faces Him in this theater of struggle which is the earth. Those who in the past have conjectured the possibility of a "conversion" of Satan at the end of time evidently have a mistaken concept regarding the evil one. If the satanic hatred against the Creator and the source that feeds him is not understood, we risk having an image of the evil one that does not grasp his intimate nature. He does not tolerate God's existence because he wants to be god in place of God. Although afraid, he rushes as to a long-desired appointment to the established place of the duel with the Messiah. Satan's rage made him launch the challenge, and his presumption caused him to hope for victory, even though he knew he was facing the Son of the Most High.

Does this representation of the tempter's pride and hateful pretension seem too audacious to you? Consider the image that the book of Revelation gives of him. Does the red dragon hesitate to devour the child just born (Rev. 12:4)? Now Satan can do nothing other than persecute the Church and her children with all the ferocity of which he is capable (Rev. 12:17). There is no doubt that when the fullness of time had arrived and the Son of God came into this world, the army of evil and its prince faced Jesus with the precise intention of defeating Him and destroying His plans for the salvation of the world.

The Son of God Prepares Himself for the Test

The way in which Jesus prepared Himself to face the adversary is striking. The temptations are preceded by moments of intense prayer and union with the Father. First, there is the participation of Jesus at the great spiritual renewal promoted by the Baptist, with the opening of the Heavens, in which there is the witness and proclamation of the Father's favor toward the Son, and the outpouring of the Holy Spirit. Then there are the forty days of fasting and prayer in the desert, during which Jesus is completely separated from the world, that is, from its words and its seductions.

We ask ourselves: Did Jesus need all of this? Jesus in His humanity needed a constant union with the will of the Father that was acquired through prayer. It is only through prayer that the tempter will be unable to separate our will from God. The evil one's success consists in alienating our hearts from the Creator. Temptation always aims to render appetizing to our free wills that which the enemy presents to the eyes of our minds. To prevent our will from being seduced, it is necessary, through prayer, to fix it on the adorable beauty of the Divine Will.

Consider the way in which Jesus faced the two most tremendous satanic assaults to which He was subject, namely, that of the desert and that of Gethsemane, recollecting Himself in an ardent and prolonged prayer. Union with God and the experience of His love gives man the discernment and strength necessary for passing the test. Jesus did not underestimate Satan. Even though in His humanity he was immune to evil, He prepared Himself for the great battle, permeating His soul with that fullness of light and strength necessary for defeating the evil one.

If the Son of God prepared Himself to face the assault of the evil one, it means that the adversary is strong and trained for war, and woe to those who are caught unprepared. Do not deceive yourself! If your soul is not vigilant and united to God, it is not possible for you to resist satanic attacks. Peter, James, and John had a bitter experience concerning this when they were invited by Jesus to be vigilant and to pray so as not to fall into temptation (Mark 14:38). The evil one is always taking aim against good people, and he patiently waits for them to lower their guard. Every day you must always be vigilant from morning to night, so that the enemy will not catch you unarmed.

Satan Studies the Prey

The biblical images of Satan are very precise and make evident his nature and his strategy. The image of the dragon illustrates his ferocity, the serpent his shrewdness, and, finally, the lion his ability as a hunter of souls. Contrary to what is frequently thought, the devil did not wait forty days before tempting Jesus. He began immediately to examine and sample his prey. It is the evangelist Luke who points out that during that entire period of prayer and fasting Jesus was tempted (Luke 4:2). It is the same evangelist who points out that Satan attacked Jesus with "every temptation" (Luke 4:13).

The tempter is a perfectionist. He analyzes people through every kind of trial to discover their various natures, tendencies, strengths, and weaknesses. The more a soul has advanced along the way of holiness, the more the evil one is constrained to study in depth her weak points. Against souls who are vigilant and protected with the armor of light (Rom. 13:12), Satan uses a strategy of continuous siege, trying them on all fronts and seeking to find even the tiniest crack to infiltrate.

Temptation is very personalized. We are often careless and do not know ourselves. We wander through a forest full of traps like carefree tourists. The evil one, however, has been following us since the age of reason and has been observing closely our tendencies, knowing us as we cannot even imagine. Once he has identified our appetites, he draws near, presenting us with the appropriate food. He behaves like every expert hunter who, for every species of animal, prepares specific bait.

Are you lustful? He presents you with a woman. Are you attached to money? He shows you an easy and dishonest way to become rich. Are you impatient? He provokes your wrath, taking advantage of the innumerable inconveniences of daily life. There is no aspect of your nature that he does not scan and scrutinize. Until he has found your dominant defect, he does not prepare the fatal trap. Not even the greatest saints are exempt from having a weak side. Do not presume that you are unable to be attacked. You face an enemy who knows everything about you and, if you are not clothed with the armor of God, he will deliver the blow to you where and when you least expect it.

After forty days and nights, the evil one realized that the regular temptations with which he lured men were ineffective with Jesus. The holy humanity of Christ offered nothing for the shrewd serpent to grip. None of the temptations that could lure common men were able to entice Jesus. However, Satan was not discouraged, and he was a long way from admitting defeat. Satan is untiring, and his pride always drives him to begin again. Have you noticed how sinners are more eager to do evil than good people are eager to do good? After Satan sized up his prey, he launched the challenge, seeking to conquer Jesus at the heart of His person and of His divine mission.

Satan Takes Advantage of Every Circumstance

The evangelists Matthew and Luke are in agreement that the great seducer waited for Jesus to be hungry before drawing near for the decisive attack. It is anything but a marginal observation, since it shows how the evil one does not neglect any particular circumstance that would be favorable to his achieving success. Satan takes advantage of a primary need of human nature, such as food, in order to use it for his subtle temptation. If he had proposed the transformation of the stones into bread at the beginning of the fast, it would have received an all too easy refusal. The shrewd serpent was patient and waited for Jesus to feel weak, hoping that he would find in His exhaustion a justification for the miracle.

The lessons that come to us from this apparently insignificant detail are many. The tempter does not omit any particular which can be used to his advantage. This is a warning for us not to grant him anything in this long, treacherous battle, in which our eternal life is at stake. Concerning this, there is a fundamental Christian virtue that comes to our assistance, namely, prudence, which is perfected and crowned by the gift of counsel. Prudence is a virtue of evaluation that enables us to weigh all the circumstances of spiritual warfare. Without prudence, we would be easily exposed to the blows of the adversary, who evaluates every action carefully before delivering the assault.

The traditional wisdom of spiritual masters unceasingly teaches that every occasion of sin must be avoided with sound judgment. Satan is perfectly aware that people who are oriented toward the good do not sin easily unless they are caught by surprise or found in situations from which it is difficult to remove themselves. He thus prepares favorable situations, without which his snares would not serve their purpose. There are countless examples regarding this, but the substance of the teaching absolutely cannot be underestimated. Oftentimes, favorable or unfavorable combinations decide the outcome of a temptation.

I remember the counsel that Bernadette, now a sister of Nevers, gave to one of her fellow sisters who was preparing to begin her apostolate as a nurse among the sick. With uncommon wisdom, she advised, "When you are with a man, always leave the door opened." Another sister, who was a great educator in the field of the recovery of drug addicts, gave instructions that even when going to Mass on Sunday, the youngsters who were still in a state of recovery should accompany one another and never be alone, because, she said, the drug dealer is always waiting in ambush, even in the surroundings of the church.

It is necessary to deny even the slightest advantage to the demon by avoiding occasions that are favorable to him. If you know that going to a place or meeting a certain person is an occasion of sin for you, then you must avoid going there or meeting that person with complete determination, because afterward, it will be too late. If you know that the content of a book or a television program will have a negative influence on you, then you must immediately decide to reject the occasion. If you foresee that in beginning to speak you will speak excessively or be led astray into destructive gossip, you must pass the time in silence.

Satan takes advantage of your fatigue, nervousness, lack of sleep, physical or psychological weakness, and even of your illness. He uses even the smallest details of your daily life to his advantage. The virtue of prudence should guide you in every circumstance. If you entrust yourself to God, it will be He Himself who will indicate to you when and where to be vigilant. It is essential that you should be like a sentry, ready to sound the alarm when danger approaches.

Satan Presents Himself as a Counselor

Before entering more deeply into the temptations, I would like to note a characteristic of the shrewdest seducer which was revealed when he confronted our first parents in the garden of Eden and is now fully manifested. He approaches the victim he has selected while presenting himself as an objective counselor. You need not be amazed. The Bible reveals to us the true nature of the evil one with the images of the serpent, the lion, and the dragon. But if he were to present himself in this guise, who would be caught by him? Thus, the rapacious wolf draws near looking like a sheep. In sheep's clothing he acts at his convenience. In the development of temptation, Satan's success depends in large part on his ability to render himself believable. He seeks to accredit himself as your friend, concerned only for your happiness and quite expert in giving you the correct counsel for acquiring it. Once he becomes your spiritual director, he can bring you where he wishes.

Satan succeeded with this game in the earthly paradise when he earned Eve's trust after having persuaded her to believe all his lies about the Word of God. He tried the same with Christ, suggesting that He begin the messianic mission by gaining the approval of the people. In effect, Satan is a great expert in the things of this world, which, in large part, is under his dominion. It certainly cannot be denied that he exercises the art of evil as no one else. The ones who are under his influence know the laws of the flesh, of egoism, and of carnal wisdom much better than the children of light, who in this field are rather artless.

Satan does not necessarily pursue his activities as a counselor directly, hissing with his lying tongue into the ears of your heart. He acts more often through the meetings in your daily life. Often his agents are your friends, acquaintances, or even your family members. Reflect on just how frequently you have been directed toward evil by someone who deceived your good faith, pretending to offer you suggestions for your good. Are there not even some parents who behave with their children as Herodias (Mark 6:24), who counseled her daughter on how to please Herod?

Unfortunately, you will find along your way many more people who will direct you on the way of the flesh rather than on the way of God. They will tell you that you are a fanatic, that you do not know how to keep up with the times, and that everyone now behaves in that manner. You should know how to discern behind their words the slimy serpent who, through the world and its formidable agents of social persuasion, distributes abundantly his counsels of degradation and perdition. Few are the ones who direct toward the good, while those who push toward evil are an immense army. But the evil ones do it with perspicacity, seeking to persuade you that they are moved by a concern for your happiness.

"If You Are the Son of God ..."

When Satan speaks, even though under the false clothes of an objective counselor, immediately notice the strident sound of the lie. Every one of his introductions contains, in very few syllables, enough poison to intoxicate all of human history. Remember the initial note with which he succeeded in charming the careless Eve: "Is it true that God said ... ?" "If you are the Son of God," he now insinuates. The lie, in the specific sense of a clever falsification of the truth, is the satanic art par excellence. When you listen to the Word of God with an open heart, it penetrates into the depths of your heart, where you hear it as the truth that it is and as the bringer of joy. When, instead, the message is a well-camouflaged error, you immediately perceive the bitter flavor and the taste of poison.

The evil one knows, although he had absolute certainty only after the Resurrection, that Jesus is the Messiah, the Son of God. The profession of faith made by the Baptist a little earlier was certainly not lost on Satan (John 1:29–34). He puts everything on the line, provoking Jesus to give a demonstration of His divine origin. The evil one's arguments correspond to the world's way of thinking. If Jesus performs miracles, He will be considered credible and worthy of faith. If He will not offer proof that the world is in a position to understand, it means that His testimony is a lie.

In this light, we understand one of the most recurring themes in the Gospels, the one regarding the certain and indisputable testimonies of Christ's divinity. The world, stirred up by the demon, wants signs that correspond to its carnal mentality. The Scribes and the Pharisees often urged Jesus to give convincing proofs of His divinity. They launched the challenge even at the foot of the Cross, asking the Crucified One to come down from the Cross so that they would be able to see and believe (Mark 15:32).

The testimonies God offers to confirm His presence and action are very different from the ones they would like. God employs the language of the Cross, a language of truth, humility, and holiness that carnal man does not comprehend, but those who have the Spirit of God understand it profoundly.

Satan asks for dazzling signs by which Jesus could confirm publicly His divine origin and mission. Since Jesus has no intention of following Satan in this direction, the liar has a ready argument: to accuse Jesus of lying and to declare His testimony null.

Supernatural signs escape the logic of the world. Changing stones into bread and throwing yourself from the Temple because the angels can support you are both ambiguous signs. They attract the attention of carnal man, but they do not necessarily convert him to God's way. Satan loves these types of signs, visual and sensational. With a spectacular display he moves the crowds, exciting their curiosity and injecting his poison, dissuading souls from the essential thing: conversion and the way of holiness.

Jesus offered only one true sign, indisputable and full of divine light, from which all the numerous miracles He performed derived their strength. It is the unrepeatable splendor and uniqueness of His sublime sanctity. No man was ever more holy or more good than Jesus. Even if He had not performed the miracles that only God can perform, the miracle of His sanctity would be enough to convince us. It is because of Jesus' sublime sanctity that we believe without any difficulty in the divine event of His Resurrection from the dead.

"Command These Stones to Become Loaves of Bread"

As we enter into the temptations of Jesus in the desert, we realize the refined art of the deceiver. He did not really have to make a big effort to seduce Adam and Eve. It is the oft-repeated deception of the evil one to offer material rewards to man to move him away from the Creator. The temptations aimed at the Messiah are much more sophisticated and touch more closely the life of the Church and the Christian experience of faith. While the temptations of Eden concern more the common man in his relationship with God, those of the desert particularly interest the believer from the standpoint of his comprehension and living of Christianity. They are two different scenarios, but they are wonderfully integrated and represent different moments of the spiritual experience.

Satan wishes to obtain irrefutable proof from Jesus of His divinity. Satan suggests a miracle, seeking to push Jesus into a messianic action directed at solving material problems. The aim is to falsify the authentic message of the Faith and to distract Jesus from His mission as redeemer. The suggestion to change the stones into bread in order to satisfy His hunger contains many snares. The most evident is that of shifting Jesus' salvific action toward materials problems, leading Him away from His essential mission, which is first and foremost the liberation from sin and evil.

This is a permanent temptation for the Church until the end of time. The Church is certainly placed in this world and shares its joys and sufferings, hopes and defeats. But her task is not to place herself on the level of solving man's material problems. The Church has always promoted the human growth of society, but her end is the eternal salvation of souls. The temptation to secularize the Church, orienting her toward human promotion and removing her from her supernatural objectives, is among the most subtle and insidious. This temptation has led many parishes and religious communities to abandon prayer, catechesis, sacrifice, and the supernatural means of apostolate as they instead involve themselves in social activities that empty the Christian presence of its meaning.

Recognition is not denied to the Church for all her social works of the past and present. But on the contrary, she is held to be useless by the world, and she is often opposed with regard to her supernatural mission of salvation. An earthly messianism, a Christianity reduced to a humanitarian religion, a Church that becomes a sort of Red Cross of the world: this is the subtle proposal of the tempter so that he can continue to dominate the world by means of unbelief and sin. A Church that does not fight spiritual and moral evil leaves the evil one undisturbed in his devastation of souls. This is exactly what he desires.

"It Is Written"

Eve took time to discuss the lie of the tempter, accepting it with a foolish carelessness that allowed it to grow in her heart until she was conquered. Jesus teaches us that the hissing of the serpent goes against the clear and resounding voice of the Word of God. Dear friend, darkness is combated by light, evil by good, and hatred by love. There is no point in debating this. When you hear around you the hissing of error, of lies, of slander, and of defamation, readily turn the eye of your mind to the Word of Truth and let it fill your heart until your heart is completely illuminated and possessed by it. When the Truth lives in you, you will pronounce the words of light which, without useless altercations, will enter the hearts of those who are in good faith and who are not obstinately closed off to the voice of God.

Consider how the evil one is forced to desist from the temptation and launch the attack from another side. He has not found a space in which he can infiltrate himself because he has encountered the One who is the Truth Himself. This can also happen to you if you are well-rooted in the Word and the sentiments of Jesus. When the lie has barely touched your ears and the seducer's music attempts to penetrate your heart, take refuge in the ivory tower of Divine Truth established in the Holy Church and keep your eyes and ears fixed only on it. How many have suffered a shipwreck of their faith because they had itching ears (2 Tim. 4:3) and took the time to listen to false prophets who, under the pretense of being apostles, help the voracious wolf to steal their souls.

"Man Shall Not Live by Bread Alone"

With the cutting sword of the Word of God, Jesus removes the mask of one of the most current and devastating satanic lies. Man is not an animal trapped in the short-term cycle of matter. He is a spiritual being who needs to find divine truth even before material food. Never before as in our time has Satan succeeded in promising happiness through material goods. The error he has promoted under the cover of a false science is that man is nothing other than a more evolved animal, fundamentally composed of matter, without a soul, without a spiritual life, without a moral law, and thus without God and eternity. Man, reduced to the hungers of his body, is born by chance and disappears into nothingness. This is the vision of life proposed by the liar who in this world succeeds in depriving man of his dignity, his beauty, his greatness, and his immortal and divine destiny.

Our society is building itself on this false assumption, fallaciously hoping that an abundance of material goods can render man happy. Satan has succeeded well in inculcating the lie that money is enough to make life worthwhile. This great illusion of opulent society is inhabited by the spirits of worry, unhappiness, and desperation. There is no future in a world built on this foundation.

Consider your life and draw the conclusions of a vision of life in which the prospect of eternity is missing. If man is only his body, and everything ends in death, what is the point of this monstrous fatigue of existence, which is filled with suffering, trials, illusions, and delusions and passes without leaving any trace, as if everything were useless?

"But by Every Word That Proceeds from the Mouth of God"

Man is not only matter, and the physical hunger of man is not his only appetite. In him there is an immortal soul which hungers for God. Uselessly man satisfies his flesh in the illusion of being happy. Only if the heart is full of the light and love of God does it overflow with peace and joy. On the one hand, Jesus uncovers the diabolic deception that identifies man solely with his body, and on the other hand, He shows to the hearts starving for eternity the living bread that satisfies hunger and the living water that quenches thirst.

Observe Jesus' great balance. He does not deny that the body has its requirements and that life in this world has its laws. He knows that our flesh is weak and needs nutrition, rest, and care. Does not the celestial Father provide food for the sparrows and clothe the lilies of the field? God cares also about our problems of daily living. Our worries regarding our daily bread, home, work, and health should be entrusted to Him. Did not Jesus take care of many sick people? Didn't He satisfy the hunger of the many people who were following Him for days to hear the Word of God?

The most shrewd serpent takes advantage of the natural and understandable concerns of man regarding the problems of daily living. He seeks to blow these worries out of proportion, as if their solution depended only upon us and God did not care about His creatures. Satan succeeds in generating anxiety about the future, robbing our hearts of peace, faith, and belief in the providence of the celestial Father. He makes you obsessed with economic or health problems, succeeding in diverting you from the most important objective of life, which is not the conservation of the body, which is destined for death, but rather the eternal beatitude of the soul.

If your principal worry is that of nurturing your soul with the truth and love of God, you can be certain that the Creator will not deny you whatever is necessary for your daily life. If you are concerned to nurture your soul, then God will provide for the needs of your body. Whoever gives to God the first place in his daily life will be assured of the divine blessing on his work and his home. If our chief worry is that of serving the Lord on the good way, all the rest will be given to us besides. To those who worry about the spiritual health of their souls, the celestial Father guarantees not only what they need at a material level but often more than what is necessary.

Watch, therefore, that the evil one does not rob you of your confidence in God, and watch that he does not drag you away into obsession with the problems of daily living. God's protection renders life safer than any material wealth.

The Devil Led Him to the Holy City

In the first temptation, you noted the subtle deception by which Satan sought, under the pretense of doing good, to make Jesus and the Church deviate from their primary mission, the eternal salvation of souls. Satan seeks to instill a false piety in which the needs of the body are blown out of proportion while those of the soul are ignored. False piety and false peace are some of the weapons used in order to deceive especially good people.

Satan uses their sentiments and takes advantage of their lack of discernment. As I was writing down these lines, I had to raise my voice with one who, because he did not want to scare a dying person with the presence of a priest, was leaving him to die without the sacraments. It was a typical example of that false piety by which Satan obtains the end for which he works, the eternal perdition of souls.

In the second temptation, Satan's action in the religious sphere, and in particular in the Church, is manifested to us. You must keep in mind that every temptation of Christ should always be seen and interpreted also in relation to the Church throughout the entire course of her history. The devil leads Jesus into the holy city and sets Him on the pinnacle of the Temple. What could be a holier or safer place? Yet the omnipresent serpent manages to slip in anywhere, even in places at the heart of the Church.

Like Christ, the Church is subject to the most subtle and satanic snares. Some of these snares are common to all men, while others are specific to the Church herself. While Jesus overcomes and defeats the evil one, the men of the Church often succumb to him. God has not granted to anyone, not even the pope, the gift of impeccability. For that reason, everyone must be vigilant in prayer and ready for spiritual warfare. Did Satan not scrutinize the twelve apostles, and did he not succeed in bringing one of them to the betrayal of his Lord?

There is a temptation which comes to the Church externally when the world pushes her to secularization, tepidity, and to the assimilation of its mentality. It is easy for you to see the devastating effects of this seduction in the empty churches, in the ministers of God who leave aside preaching the truths of the Faith that are thought to be uncomfortable, in the absence of prayer, in the yielding to current fashions, and in the tolerance of immorality.

There also exists a series of temptations that come from within the Church. These temptations aim to adulterate and corrupt the authentic religious experience. A popular saying states that Satan often disguises himself as a friar. What is the meaning of this saying, which at first glance seems improbable and surprising? The wisdom of the simple folk warns us to be on guard against false representations of religion and against its shrewd and exploitative uses for bad purposes. We might not like it, but the fact is that even individual men of the Church can deceive, and they do it with shrewdness, dressed in the appropriate clerical garb. Thus, vigilance must be doubled.

"If You Are the Son of God, Throw Yourself Down"

Satan invites Jesus to cast Himself down from the height of the Temple's pinnacle and entrust His safety to the angels, who would bear Him up on their hands so that the people would see and believe. Here, too, is an evident attempt to distract Jesus from His mission as the redeemer, which He intends to realize through the humiliation of the Cross. Will the people not later ask Christ to come down from the Cross so that they may have faith in Him (Mark 15:32)? God's way of saving the world is one of humility, silence, hiding, sacrifice, the gift of self, and expiatory suffering. Satan, however, loves a spectacle, success, glory, and applause. If Christ has chosen the Cross, Satan has chosen the stage.

As long as this seduction is limited to the world, it is not, as such, a danger for the Church. The emptiness of the vanity fair in which many men move like inconsistent ghosts is palpable. There are some men who, if they do not succeed in making even a small mark in the changing carousel of this world, feel they have not lived. The French philosopher Descartes affirmed, "I think, therefore I am." Today, if you do not play at least the role of an extra on the stage of the earth, you may convince yourself that you do not exist, and perhaps you lament, saying that God has forgotten you.

When the craze of playing a public role enters the Church, it makes religion a spectacle. It is a very current temptation which needs attentive reflection. The Christian religion is great and beautiful, not in the worldly sense but rather in the supernatural meaning of the word. It has a purity and a modesty that instinctively leads her not to exhibit herself uselessly to the world.

To give a public witness, to preach to the far ends of the earth, to be a shining lamp on the candelabra are certainly evangelical commands, but they are also for people whom God does not hesitate to burden with the Cross and to subject to humiliation and persecution.

All this is something very different from the temptation of making religion one ingredient among the many others of the vanity fair. Why are so many priests invited onto television if not to make of them extras in a world now reduced to a stage on which men enter and exit like shoe heels on an assembly line? Religion that exhibits itself, religion that prefers publicity spots or commercials to preaching, religion that seeks showy signs, the religion of gurus and not of saints, has nothing to do with the way of the Cross that Christ endured. In all of these, we have the constantly repeated satanic falsification of religion.

The search for sensational things and for miracles deserves a particular reflection. God has worked and continues to work miracles, many more than we are disposed to believe. He works them above all in the spiritual order, when He revives those whose lives were destroyed and manifests the miracle of goodness and sanctity in callous sinners.

God works miracles even in the material order, in the hidden textures of daily life where He defends and protects us. Through the paternal concern of His providence, He assures us of our daily food. He takes care of our work, families, and health, defending us from the innumerable snares of the world and of the evil one.

Who perceives these miracles? Only the true friends of God, who have the clear eyes of faith. Many do not know how to see these miracles and seek some flashy phenomena, confusedly thinking that only extravagant and even dangerous manifestations are supernatural. Behind such manifestations is often hidden the one who asked Jesus to exhibit Himself in a useless, clownish act merely to obtain the applause of the world.

In this religion that is made a show is also evident the false holiness of those who exhibit themselves to the gullible and who act the part of the saint but do not live it. We will consider this subject in depth, and we will treat the question of false prophets later. For now, it is enough that you understand that sanctity that is presented as in a theater is the perfect realization of the satanic lie. It is better to be a great sinner than a false saint. The first deceives only himself, while the second deceives and seduces many weak souls.

Remember, dear friend, that true religion is humble, chaste, and crucified. The miracles of God are not like those the world loves and seeks. The miracles of saints are very different from those of false or of hypocritical "saints." Wait for the miracles of God and ask for them in the fervor of prayer. But do not run to wherever they are exhibited like circus phenomena.

Satan Cites the Bible

I would like you to note a typical particularity about this temptation. Satan, who in the first act was silenced by Jesus with a citation from the Word of God, now faces Jesus with the same weapon, citing the Bible to him. "It is written," the perfidious serpent dares to say. Are you amazed? You should not be. Think of the many errors the liar has disseminated throughout the course of history with false interpretation of the Bible. The Word of God cited in this way, but counterfeited and interpreted at one's own pleasure, has been in the past and is still today one of the favorite activities of the demon.

There is no heretic, schismatic, apostate, or enemy of the Church who does not make reference to the Bible to justify his own position. Recently, even some intellectuals, atheists, and materialists, with the objective of denying the existence of the soul and of the afterlife, have made recourse to the authority of Sacred Scripture. To sustain their thesis that man is merely an advanced animal, they quote the passage in which man is reminded that he is dust and to dust he shall return (Gen. 3:19). The panorama is now complete. Rebellious man now uses the Bible to combat revealed doctrine.

On the streets of your city, or of your village, or at the door of your house, you are met by zealous missionaries who evangelically proceed two by two and ask you to read and discuss the Bible with them. After you have listened to them drone about this or that text, they conclude that the Holy Trinity does not exist, that Jesus Christ is the archangel Michael, that, naturally, the Madonna is not a virgin, because all the numerous brothers of Jesus are listed in the Bible, etc. It is, as you yourself can recognize, the destruction of the Christian Faith in the name of the Bible, which the missionaries cite in the very style of the devil, who uses Scripture for his own use and consumption.

Be on guard against the satanic use of the Bible, in which the Word of God is falsely interpreted and often even consciously counterfeited to sustain errors. Sacred Scripture was born in the womb of the Church by the work of the Holy Spirit, just as Christ was conceived in the womb of the Virgin Mary by the power of the Holy Spirit. The Church and the Holy Spirit have generated the Word of God, and only they can interpret it in its true, supernatural sense.

Do Not Use God for Your Purposes

The tempter invites Jesus to throw Himself down from the pinnacle of the Temple because the angels would sustain Him; but Jesus responds again with a dry and cutting reply, contrasting the light of divine truth to Satan's error: "It is written, you shall not tempt the Lord your God." It is a response filled with meaning and teaching for all those who believe in God and work in the Church but expose themselves to the temptation of using religion to serve their own egotistical purposes.

The command not to tempt God implies above all the refutation of spectacular miracles. God is humble, and the signs of His presence do not occur according to the pride and vainglory of man. God does not desire to work miracles without true usefulness or according to the whims of men. In the divine governance of the world, a miracle is always an intervention of the Creator's wisdom, and He does not abuse His omnipotence. When He works, He tends ordinarily to give great value to His creatures without replacing them with Himself.

For example, if God intends to listen to your prayer in which you ask to be healed of an illness, He does not necessarily do it with an action that takes the place of the natural course of events. Instead, He helps you to find a doctor who gives you a correct diagnosis and administers the appropriate medicine. If you ask God to help you find a job, you cannot, having prayed, sit back and expect that a letter of employment will appear. You must busy yourself in the search for a job. The more active and confident you are, the more God will help you. God gives value and responsibility to His creatures and does not desire to do Himself what they themselves can and must do. If you, having prayed to the angel of God, prepare to make a car trip, your prayer will certainly not exempt you from the necessity of driving with attention and observing the norms of safety.

Man tempts God every time he asks God to act in situations caused by his own foolishness and irresponsibility and every time he desires to provoke God's miraculous intervention. However, this temptation has still darker and more disquieting aspects to it. It touches the very roots of the mission of Jesus and the Church. Jesus and the Church have come to serve and not to be served. The temptation of using God for one's own glory, rather than serving Him and declaring afterward that one is only an unworthy servant, is perhaps the subtlest of the temptations against Jesus. It has great application in the lives of the men of the Church and in the lives of the common faithful.

Now it is clear to you how Satan aims to pervert religion in the second temptation. The objective of Satan in the first temptation was to eliminate the religious dimension of life in the name of material well-being, but in the second temptation, Satan plans to falsify the religious experience in itself. The great seducer realizes that man is "naturally religious," as the ancients affirmed. The devil's objective of eliminating religion and destroying the Church is not to be gained even though he desires it with all of his strength. Thus, he seeks to alter religion so that it becomes an instrument of corruption rather than one of salvation.

The evil one achieves this objective in many ways. Even in the first Christian communities, the apostle John recognized the presence of the "synagogue of Satan," as he called it (Rev. 2:9). Groups of dubious inspiration have always been hidden in the folds of the vestments of Christ's spouse. Identifying and unmasking them is not easy. Now more than ever they are hidden in the ecclesiastical thicket and are much more numerous than one may think. They feed on deceptive doctrines that are more apt to satisfy their spiritual gluttony than to lead them in an authentic way of sanctity.

From this perspective, religion is distorted. Instead of elevating man to God, it becomes an ingredient for satisfying the "self." It can happen in an even greater way to the ministers of the Church. Instead of serving with loyalty, sincerity, dedication, and a spirit of sacrifice toward God and souls, they may make use of their positions and offices to satisfy their hunger for glory, honor, and money, with all the naturally connected vices.

To all those who make use of God and of the Church for their own benefit, Jesus issues a strong rebuke, presenting the divine commandment: "You shall not tempt the Lord your God." Know, dear friend, that it is less grave to deny God than to try to take advantage of Him for your own purposes. A person without religion can always desire light from the depths of his darkness. But what standing before God has the person who tries to take advantage of Him instead of serving Him with a sincere and pure heart? Can he still turn to the One whom he has daily abused?

Above all, it is the ministers of the Church who must be vigilant, because Satan does entice them and succeeds in leading them astray. Woe to them if they do not know how to present a pure and authentic religion to their faithful. A hypocritical pastor cannot guide the flock in the way of sanctity. A preacher who is unfaithful in doctrinal matters offers poisonous food to his people. A minister who does not believe in God murders souls. If the evil one seduces the pastor, the consequences for the sheep are terrible. Woe to those communities that have a mercenary instead of a pastor and in consequence are exposed to the ferocity of the rapacious wolves (John 10:12).

"The Devil ... Showed Him All the Kingdoms of the World"

The third temptation, in which the demon promises all the power and glory of all the kingdoms of the world to the Messiah, reveals to us more fully the deep roots of the rebellious angel's sin and the reason for his radical opposition to God. He requests for himself that adoration that is an exclusive prerogative of the Most High and which can never be attributed to a creature for any reason whatsoever. At the same time, Satan also claims a power over society that does not belong to him. Even though it is true that the demon exercises a great influence over society through sin, this power is always subject to the governance of God over the world.

Before entering more thoroughly into the third temptation, which shows Satan's desire to take God's place in the heart of man, it is necessary to pause and reflect on the ability of the ancient serpent to make use of creatures, to seduce them, and to drive them far away from their Creator. Satan wants above all to tempt Christ with the mirage of a political messianism that aspires to the acquisition of power and glory. It is a temptation Jesus will have to reject on many occasions throughout the course of His public life, particularly when the flock will seek to proclaim Him king.

He dismisses this messianism with decisiveness and strength, just as he also rejected a messianism based on spectacular religion in which miracles, which are meant to manifest the grace of God, are instead used only to amaze and attract the applause of the crowd. Jesus is King, but of hearts, and His throne is the Cross, while the weapons of His conquest are those of truth and love.

There is no doubt that until the end of the world, the Church will be put under the same form of seduction. How many times are we tempted to support ourselves by the false strength of the world or to use human weapons to acquire spiritual ends? It is an extremely insidious temptation against which the Church can never be vigilant enough. The strength and the efficacy of the Church in this world comes from God alone. The Church must not only be able to follow the way of poverty, simplicity, and human weakness already endured by our Lord but must also never be entirely surprised if she receives more persecution than approval from the world. The more the Church is faithful to the Gospel, the more she will be opposed.

Persecution renders the Church strong and keeps her faithful. Worldly support weakens her, softens her, and takes her away from her mission. This is why Satan is always ready to offer this support in abundance. Consider, dear friend, how God offers to the Son the Cross, while Satan offers riches, glory, and power. This also happens with all of us. God glorifies us through the Cross, but Satan destroys us with what he offers before our eyes. The gifts of the serpent are always full of poison for whoever accepts them.

"All These I Will Give You . . ."

You have already seen the demon presenting himself in the disguise of a counselor who is totally concerned with your happiness. Now you see him disguised as the benefactor who generously gives you everything in the world. Naturally, his aim is always the same. With what he offers you, he wishes to attract you to himself to dominate you. Everything Satan presents to our appetites is bait to capture us. The aim of all his approaches is to rule our souls forever.

Nevertheless, Satan shamelessly lies when he claims that the kingdoms of the world with their power and glory have been put into his hands. It is true that Jesus calls him the "prince of this world," but this expression is limited to the hearts of men who have refuted the kingship of God and accepted that of the evil one. Sacred Scripture unceasingly celebrates the lordship of the Most High over the world, human history, and the activity of the tempter. Even though Satan's activity is intense and at times impressive, it always remains under the power of God, who, even when He permits evil, does it to obtain the best possible good.

Thus, God alone reigns, and even Satan is forced in spite of himself to accomplish the plans of the Omnipotent. Nevertheless, Satan succeeds in deceiving many, presenting himself as a great patron who offers generously, apparently without claiming anything in return. There are many who think that only the shrewd, the cunning, and the dishonest succeed in this world, while those who desire to keep their heart pure and follow the upright and honest way are bound to fail. For this reason, many are tempted to abandon God and will not omit any means, even the most immoral ones, to gain success in the world.

Dear friend, things are not this way. If you look back in history, you will see that saints and good men have remained in the memory and veneration of men, while the violent, arrogant, and corrupt end up in history's garbage bin. Our God, as the humble maiden of Nazareth sings, is He who throws the powerful off their thrones and raises up the humble. He is the Lord who satisfies the poor with good things, while He sends the rich away empty-handed.

Satan tempts you, insinuating to you that to succeed in this world, you must accept its laws based on strength, arrogance, shrewdness, and deception. He wishes to convince you that without his help, you will not be able to succeed in society. Yet there is a popular proverb that refutes this, "Ill-gotten gains are scattered by the devil." On the contrary, God blesses uprightness and honesty. If you are faithful to God and walk on the straight path, He will protect your work, your profession, and even your activities in the higher responsibilities of social, economic, and political life.

"… If You Will Fall Down and Worship Me"

Satan wants to steal man from God because he desires to obtain his adoration. He hates God and does not accept being a creature. He wishes to be God, but he is unable. This is the source of his rebellion and his desire to create his own kingdom as an alternative to the divine kingdom. His highest aspiration is to obtain from man the worship and adoration the creature must render to his Creator alone.

Nevertheless, there is an abysmal difference between the adoration given to God and that directed toward the demon. In the adoration given to the living and true God, the creature is fulfilled and becomes a participant in the divine life. In the humility of submission, the servant becomes a son and inherits in Jesus and with Jesus. In satanic adoration, the creature is made a slave of a proud and hateful tyrant and becomes a participant in Satan's wretchedness and in his eternal desperation. The adorer of Satan receives Satan in recompense.

In order to make himself adored, the demon displays a strength and power that in reality he does not possess. When he claims that all the power and glory of the kingdoms of the world have been put into his hands and that he can give them to whomever he desires, he is shamelessly lying. When men choose to adore Satan, they do not possess the world but instead are possessed by the evil one. Yet whoever belongs to Christ participates in His lordship over all creation, as the apostle Paul emphasizes many times.

Dear friend, you must never forget that Satan seeks to impress men with a power that he does not possess. His strength is undeniable, and he succeeds in seducing many men. Nevertheless, his power is nothing compared to the omnipotence of Christ. Even Satan's successes are utilized by God, in ways often unknown to us, to accomplish God's designs for salvation. Was not the Cross, designed by the hatred of Hell, the very instrument for the salvation of the world? The strength of the evil one is freely given to him by man. If man desired it, through the simple invocation of a prayer, he could put into flight all the powers of evil. This is witnessed in the lives of many saints.

Do not be impressed by the haughtiness of the liar who would like you to believe that evil is unavoidable, that sin is stronger than grace, and that the world is in his hands. It is true that sin abounds in the world, but the Blood of Christ and the mercy of God also flow into the world. God knows that man sins and that Satan triumphs over many lives, but the victory of God is the conversion of the sinner. Although Satan is exalted through sin, God rejoices and is victorious with the new life of grace.

The world is not under the sun of Satan but is covered by the omnipotent love of God, whose light knows no end. The sanctity that flourishes in every historical period on earth is the witness of the divine victory over the false strength of evil. The frightening monotony of sin that corrodes every man may cause you to think that no one is able to escape the coils of the slimy serpent. Actually, there are very few who succeed in keeping their baptismal innocence throughout their entire lives. Nevertheless, grace is triumphant every time man is reborn, and the most weighty victories of God are those in which callous sinners become great saints.

"Begone, Satan!"

The "Begone, Satan!" pronounced by Jesus is the victory of the New Adam that begins the time of grace of the kingdom of God over the heart of man. When Satan tempts, man is attracted by what is offered to him. For the attraction to be broken and the temptation dissolved, the words "I renounce" must resound strongly and clearly in the heart. There is a lordship in Jesus that is not in us. Temptation never even touched His heart, which overflows with the infinite love of the Father. We can say the same about the temptation that the envious serpent aimed toward the holy and immaculate Virgin. Even the saints who purified their spirits through the incandescent fire of spiritual warfare learned to give a flawless refutation to the allurements of the tempter.

It is not easy for the majority of men to renounce that which Satan presents to their carnal "selves" and which is often hidden under a mask of false respectability. It is in temptation that we are revealed to ourselves as what we are. Our hidden complicities with evil are brought to light, and little serpents, which wander about in the labyrinth of our self-consciousness, open up their greedy mouths. Satan attracts you to himself by these appetites, and if you do not make a heartfelt effort to decapitate them, you will not come out the victor.

The spiritual tradition has coined a meaningful expression. The word *mortification*, so loathed these days, means "to put to death." What needs to be put to death? The living and extremely tenacious tendencies of our egotistical "self," on which Satan works to make us, his desired prey, enter into temptation so that he can assail us. The will must cut like an axe at the roots of evil in us until they are severed. You must *decide* to renounce. The word *decide*[6] indicates the act of chopping with an axe blow.

All of this takes a heavy effort on our part. When evil tendencies have become strong through having been cultivated and nourished, it is not easy to sever them with the first blow. Often this effort takes time, but in the end, grace triumphs. The unequivocal sign of victory is when you are in a position to renounce what Satan puts in front of your eyes. This will be possible for you if spiritual discernment has put you in a position to see the trap. When a fish realizes that a morsel is merely bait, it goes away without returning. For the will to decide with clarity and resolution, you must discover the insidiousness of the serpent in the light of grace. How can you eat a piece of fruit you know is poisonous? In prayer, the insidiousness is perceived and renunciation is decided. The temptation vanishes, and Satan goes away.

"Angels . . . Ministered to Him"

There is an end to temptation. Satanic assaults are governed by the powerful hand of God, who decides both the intensity and the duration of the test. Of course, if your no to Satan is not loud and clear from the beginning, then there are some complicities in you. If the tempter perceives even the smallest crack through which he can infiltrate himself into your heart, his assaults are constantly renewed with increasing ferocity until you are finally dragged away into the bog of his enticements and enchantments. Little by little, he will swallow you until you have suffocated.

[6] From the Latin *decidere*, "to cut off."

When the evil one realizes that you are wide awake and vigilant and that your will is a fortified wall of steel without cracks, he leaves you and prepares himself for another moment, when he hopes to surprise you in the sleep of tepidity and negligence. The Gospel tells us that after every defeat, an individual demon arms himself for even more violent assaults, calling to his assistance even worse demons (Luke 11:26).

Nevertheless, when you, like Jesus, resound your "Begone, Satan," you live in a unique moment filled with joy and glory. We poor creatures are not able to pronounce a phrase so commanding that it manifests the grandeur and the divine dignity of Christ. We must more modestly say, "I renounce," turning the eyes of our mind from the abyss of our misery to our God and Lord, who renews our absolute will with obedience and with a desire to serve with all the love of our little hearts.

The Gospels recount that after the victory of Christ over the demon, the angels drew near to serve Him. Allow me to tell you that something similar happens to every Christian. Our little victories over the evil one are always a participation in the divine victory of Jesus Christ. At the same time, these little victories are also a participation in His glory and in the joy of Heaven, which rejoices over each soul that converts and walks with determination on the road to sanctity.

You will not find in any other part of life the joy that is experienced in the victory over temptation. When you renounce evil, it will seem to you that you are losing something that you absolutely cannot do without. Satan has tormented you thus far with a thirst which he caused to rise up in you, yet when you renounce the dead water he has offered you, suddenly a fountain of pure and inexhaustible water will gush up from the bottom of your heart, giving you eternal life.

12

The Beginning of Temptation

Satan Prepares the Terrain

Having considered two great biblical scenes in which the Word of God reveals to us the seduction of the evil one and at the same time the means to reject it, we will now analyze more thoroughly the human experience of temptation as it emerges from the reflections and the teachings of spiritual masters and from the lives of the saints. In this field, we all have personal experience on which to meditate and from which there is much to learn. It is a sphere in which both doctrine and life enlighten each other in an extraordinary way. All men who are open to the problems of spirituality must feel personally involved and personally called to ponder these matters.

Satan is not a hunter who randomly roams through the forest in the hope of casually coming across his game. From the two great biblical temptations emerges an image of a being who is intelligent, shrewd, and cautious. He calculates every move, accurately pondering every word and dealing his blow at the opportune moment with great strength and perfidy. From a certain point of view, temptation is a masterpiece. Intelligence, lies, calculations, deceptions, and ferocity form an explosive mixture. The attack has excellent planning, and the results are often deadly. The adversary, dear friend, towers over you, and it is only with the light and the strength of God that you will be able to come away from the attack unscathed.

I would like to begin by saying that Satan loves difficult prey. Certainly, he is not as the hunter of mushrooms who, tired and depressed, turns back, content to fill his basket with the common mushrooms he can find in his own backyard. The evil one considers easy prey as already his. Holding them by the leash of their own vices, he is certain that they will never go far away.

Satan instead seeks those persons who are committed to the spiritual life. When he crept into the earthly paradise, Adam and Eve were clothed with the splendor of grace. He did not hesitate to face Christ, from whom emanates the fullness of divine sanctity. He circled the apostolic college, finally seducing the one who would be the traitor. The more advanced a person is in the way of perfection, and the more spiritual responsibility he has, the more the tempter studies, besieges, and assaults him until he has obtained victory.

Every temptation is uniquely prepared. Like all hunters, Satan seeks to surprise his prey, taking advantage of a favorable moment when the prey is unarmed and not paying attention. He knows that if he faces you in a moment of spiritual fervor, he will have great difficulty in succeeding. He begins ahead of time and prepares his trap from far away, without your noticing him. When temptation comes, the net has already been woven in absolute silence, and from the very beginning, you are in a disadvantageous situation.

The shrewd serpent begins by disarming you. The weapon of your victory and of his defeat is the fervor of prayer. He will approach you in an indirect way and with great patience until you fall into tepidity, so that your prayers will no longer render

God present in your life. You are without the light of discernment and the strength of a good will. Perhaps Satan will not succeed in stopping you from prayer entirely, but it is enough for him that the remaining prayers are innocuous, like fragile and blunt weapons that break into pieces upon impact. If you are disarmed, how can you defend yourself against the mouth of the lion?

Having taken away your weapons of battle, Satan then seeks to weaken you. The demon is perfectly aware that he will never immediately succeed in bringing a person who is strengthened by the grace of God to commit a mortal sin. And so he makes great efforts to make small openings in the fortress of the soul. He will first make you ignore some imperfections, then he will lead you to justify some weaknesses. Afterward, he will make you accept real, venial sins. In this way, your will loses the pure and ardent flames of love, and you begin to consider the distance between light and grave sin. Now you are in a situation of great fragility, and it is enough for Satan to dangle the bait before you at the right moment for you to fall into temptation.

Satan Sets the Trap

In temptation, the seducer offers evil under the guise of good. No one would accept evil if it were recognized as such. The human will has a natural tendency toward good. First it recognizes good and then it chooses it. It is very difficult for a human being to come to the luciferian awareness of desiring evil for the sake of evil, simply in hatred and rebellion against God. The demon, to be successful, must study the way to present the disobedience of God's commandments as a possibility for happiness. When he is more persuasive, he has more success. The satanic trap consists in preparing the bait in the best ways to attract you to himself without your noticing him.

The Deceiver

Sin is always something filthy and degrading. The extraordinary ability of the seducer consists in rendering sin beautiful and desirable to our eyes. In the storm of temptation, you must keep in mind the ugliness of sin, as God has shown you in particular moments of grace. The evil one will play his malicious music, seeking to penetrate your heart and seduce it with his enchanting notes. The great Homer represented well this existential situation in the tale of *The Odyssey* when Ulysses binds himself to the mast of the ship to resist the seductive song of the sirens.

Rendering sin beautiful is the supreme art of the great spellbinder. There is nothing more nauseating, horrible, and deleterious. The notable influence the demon exercises in our times can be inferred from the fact that many sins are exalted as forms of freedom and of fulfilling oneself. Only a society blinded by the evil one could affirm that poison is good for you. Think, for example, about the public promotion, and even exaltation, of sexual degeneration and perversions of which even pagans were ashamed.

When temptation rages, the able spellbinder will present evil to you as an entirely desirable good. In a particular way, money, sex, power, prestige, glory, and even violence and vengeance appear to you as objects that you could in no way renounce. In the hands of the unsurpassable deceiver, even a little piece of glass will glitter as a diamond, which you will do anything to have, even ruin yourself. Does it not happen like this to so many people?

Evil masquerading as good is the bait without which the trap does not spring. The bait, however, is not everything. Satan seeks to situate the trap in the most favorable frame possible. He takes care of the places, circumstances, and occasions of temptation. Everything is studied in the most minute details, and nothing is left unexamined.

The demon knows that certain places are particularly propitious for seducing. Even more so, many of them are quite proximate occasions of sin. Think, for example, about bars or nightclubs. Some deceive themselves that there is nothing evil in spending a Saturday night at one of these establishments. Yet, is it not true that in those places, sex, drugs, alcohol, deafening music, empty conversation, obscene language, and compromising encounters are instruments in the hands of the evil one, used all too easily to degrade souls?

Even more than places, Satan uses different persons very shrewdly for his purposes. God has His faithful, but Satan also has those who serve him. At times they are aware of it, at other times they are not, but they are equally useful for his purposes. Think back over your life until you reach the innocent years of your childhood, and try to remember how many times you were initiated into evil by the advice, behavior, or complicity of companions. Although it is true that you must thank God for the holy persons whom He had you meet, know that the seducer also organizes his meetings. On many occasions, there are men who will attempt to entice you to do evil. Satan uses them with an extraordinary ability. The danger is maximized when they come to you as good people who want to advise and help you.

The demon attentively examines, in addition to people and places, even the circumstances in which he sets the temptation. I have already told you that he knows how to wait for the right moment when you are tired, discouraged, lazy in prayer, or tepid in the spiritual life. He takes into account even external circumstances so that the temptation reaches you when you are unprepared and not expecting it. Taking the prey by surprise is an advantage which is too great for a hunter to renounce. The evil one moves about in absolute silence, alert and perfectly camouflaged. When he draws near to deceive you, you do not suspect anything. When the demon is discovered, and you are aware of his action, his threat is very minor.

I remember searching for mushrooms in the forest when I was a boy and, on several occasions, discovering dangerous vipers lurking nearby. I would see them close to my hands and feet while going up a slope covered with leaves. A chill would run through my entire body when I would think of the danger I had just left behind. I could have unknowingly leaned a hand on the silent reptile and been bitten. But once he is singled out, the viper is no longer dangerous. The same happens with the infernal serpent, who is insidious until you see him but loses his advantage when you unmask him.

The Hissing of the Serpent

There is a precise moment in which temptation springs up. It is presented to the mind as an attractive thought. Satan, before entering your heart with the permission of your free will, must knock at the door of your mind. Every temptation begins with a thought that goes through your mind or an image which strikes your fancy. God permits the evil one to surprise us, acting upon our capacity to know things, but He never allows Satan to penetrate our souls without the consent of our free will.

The book of Daniel recounts the story of two old judges who habitually saw the young Susanna, a woman of rare beauty who feared God, walking through her husband's garden. One day, the horrible thought suddenly entered their minds: Why not take advantage of the occasion in which Susanna takes her bath alone in the garden by approaching her and forcing her to lie with us (see Dan. 13)?

The moment in which an evil thought penetrates your mind is exactly the moment in which the serpent attacks with his mortal bite. Naturally, Satan had already prepared everything beforehand, exploiting the occasions and taking care of every circumstance. However, there is a very specific instant in which he comes into the open and delivers the blow with precision. This is the moment in which the thought of fulfilling some evil deed sparkles in front of the eyes of your mind. This is the fatal moment in which the temptation is initiated.

Naturally, in this phase, sin has not been committed. At this moment, you are merely the victim of an assault that you could still victoriously reject. Often, the thoughts with which Satan assails us come in massive formations with which he tortures and beats us. At times, a person is oppressed by the perversity and obscenity of images that assail him without any rest. One even wonders: Is it possible that such horrible things of this kind come only to my mind? Dear friend, be consoled; think about the fact that even the saints, already well advanced on the way of perfection, have had experiences similar to yours.

The effects of the satanic assault are quickly felt. When temptation begins, you are overtaken by a great uneasiness. Your entire being begins to tremble, losing all previous tranquility and serenity. Satan is insistent and untiring. You feel him moving around, seeking to remove your peace and attacking you from every side. He wraps you in a shroud of darkness and oppression. He draws you into a disquieting vortex of agitation which has often worn down even the greatest spiritual athletes. In such moments, confide in a confessor or in a person who can offer you valid relief.

The thought of evil that Satan thrusts before the eyes of our minds is like bait that awakens our hidden appetites. The little serpents that are hidden in us greedily open up their mouths upon seeing what the evil one is offering. At the sight of Susanna, and at the possibility of being alone with her in the garden, the two old men, notes the book of Daniel, are on fire with passion to the point of losing the use of reason. Temptation shakes our being, bringing to light everything which broods in the depths of our unconscious.

It is in these situations that every one of us can know himself as he truly is, without pretense and deception. A bank employee once told me about something that happened while he was working. Two thieves were robbing the bank, and while they were attempting to escape, they had left the safe opened, and quite a bit of money was left behind. This employee, who was alone and very close to the safe at that time, was surprised to find himself thinking: why not take advantage of the situation and take a little bit of the money? After all, no one would have known. The thought was readily rejected, but the point is that temptation comes swiftly, and the most dishonest thoughts can shake even the most honest people. It is exactly in this type of situation that man knows the truth about himself.

As you have understood and certainly experienced, temptation is a moment of intense suffering and dismay. Satan assaults the bastions of the mind from every side with insistent and hammering thoughts, causing our appetites, ambitions, and aggressiveness to boil, bringing out the darker and more turbid layers of our being. In cases of weakness or of psychological illness, the satanic thought becomes an obsession which remains at our side and from which one is unable to free himself.

Even if a person is very much disturbed and afflicted, in this phase, there is no way that we can state that the person has committed sin. At times, the cloud of dust raised by the tempter is so thick that it is difficult for you to establish whether or not

Satan has been successful in opening a breach in your heart and in obtaining the consent of your will. Know, however, that inasmuch as you have not deliberately ceded to the temptation, embracing the seducer's offer and appropriating it to yourself, you are not yet defeated.

There exists a door that Satan seeks to break through to proclaim victory. It is not the door of the mind, from which he enters and exits whenever he wishes. It is the door of the heart, to which only you and God possess the key. It is the key of free will. If Satan is to settle in your heart and become your leader, you must decide to open the door. All the plans of the evil one, all the force he displays, all the suggestions, images, and thoughts he presents are to persuade you to open this door.

Dear friend, understand that if you do not want Satan to capture you, he simply cannot. He is a thief, but he cannot enter the home of your heart without your knowledge and consent. The crux of the problem is that you must not be convinced by him to open the door.

13

The Dynamics of Temptation

Temptation Is Not Superior to Our Strength

I have already explained to you that Satan is not omnipotent and cannot do whatever he wants. Nevertheless, the weakness of the flesh, the complexity of the world, and the action of the evil one can create situations in which you despair of victory. In every human battle, even in a battle of spiritual dimensions, the psychological component is fundamental, and Satan exploits it to his advantage. If the enemy is successful in making you overestimate him, convincing you that he is the strongest, he obtains a noteworthy advantage. It is not rare that many people, even from the very first skirmish, throw in the towel and are overcome because they are persuaded that it is useless to resist an adversary who towers over them.

Regarding this, it is necessary to have firm faith convictions, solidly grounded on the Word of God. Although Satan is powerful, God is all-powerful. The grace of Christ is the divine strength that God gives to all those who ask for it in prayer. With this strength, the good will of man can defeat the evil one. Any representation of the spiritual combat in which the strength of Christ is doubted must be rejected as false and dangerous. The immense multitude of saints, in the sense of all those who are clothed with sanctifying grace, testifies that victory over the evil one is possible.

St. Paul gave very precise reassurance about the spiritual battle to Christians at Corinth, and, of course, to all of us, writing: "No temptation has overtaken you that is not common to man. God is faithful, and he will not let you be tempted beyond your strength, but with the temptation will also provide the way of escape, that you may be able to endure it" (1 Cor. 10:13). Although it is true that Satan is waiting in ambush, it is also true that God guards and protects us. No one can think that the victory over the demon resides in his own personal strength. The overestimation of one's own strength is an opening into which the shrewd serpent immediately creeps. Our confidence resides in the fidelity of God, who never abandons His children.

Jesus, in the tremendous hour of darkness, prayed to the Father for His disciples, asking not that they would be taken from the world but that they would be protected from the evil one (John 17:15). This prayer of Jesus is offered for every one of us and is the true guarantee of our victory. If we are well connected to the Lord like the branches to the vine, the storm of evil will never be able to tear us away from Him. The apostle John wrote words of great encouragement and comfort about this: "We know that any one born of God does not sin, but He who was born of God keeps him, and the evil one does not touch him. We know that we are of God, and the whole world is in the power of the evil one" (1 John 5:18–19).

These certitudes of faith must be part of the weapons with which the believer faces the moment of the test. Once a temptation has begun, the enemy will seek to create a situation so difficult that you may be induced to believe that it is impossible to resist. It is enough for you to think about the tremendous test of Gethsemane, where Jesus was assailed with such great fear and anguish that He became saddened unto death, so that His sweat became drops of Blood that fell to the earth.

Certainly, at that moment, the dragon had vomited all of his poison out against Christ, well aware of the fact that it was a decisive battle. Nevertheless, Satan is no less ferocious in front of us, knowing well the value of even one soul in the eyes of God. At the moment of temptation, Satan often raises up a frightening storm to terrify us. He assaults us with thoughts, images, and fears that appear to us absolutely without foundation once the temptation vanishes. He enlarges problems, amplifies dangers, and excites our appetites, seeking to convince us that if we do not eat the fruit he offers us, it will not be possible for us to live. Our surrender is his goal. To obtain this aim, he hits us with a storm of discouraging thoughts to induce us to abandon the struggle. He darkens our minds to make us think that God has abandoned us and that defeat is now inevitable.

St. Ignatius of Loyola tells the story in his autobiography of the beginning of his conversion, when he went to Manresa for a long period of prayer in total isolation from the world. It was there that Satan appeared to him in the form of a false angel of light and sought to dissuade him from the path he had begun, saying to him: "You are only thirty-five years old; how will you make it to seventy, following a life of such penance and renunciation?" The evil one, as you see, attacks with discouragement, seeking to persuade you that the way of God is beyond your strength. In this way, he easily succeeds in many temptations, because he makes you surrender under his first blows.

In the moment of the storm, therefore, hold firmly in your heart the conviction that you will be able to reject with the grace of Christ whatever assaults the evil one launches. Even though you are fragile, never forget that the power of God is manifested in our weakness. The confidence that you can be victorious even in the most violent temptations resides in the strength that comes from the grace of Christ.

Temptation Has a Determined Time

In the strict sense of the word, satanic temptation has a determined time. Satan tempts us throughout our lives, multiplying his efforts as we advance in the spiritual warfare. God, however, decrees that the assaults of the evil one should not be incessant. Moments of great struggle are followed by necessary oases of restoration and peace. We know this first and foremost from our personal experiences with daily battle. When the demon, having worked in secret to prepare the soil, comes into the open, we are immediately aware of his dark presence of unrest and insidiousness. The evangelist Luke confirms this in recounting the temptations of Jesus: "And when the devil had ended every temptation, he departed from him until an opportune time" (Luke 4:13).

Nevertheless, vigilance must never cease, even when the devil is defeated and momentarily leaves the field. The root of evil is in us, at the base of our wounded hearts, and around us, in a world in which we find on every street corner an incentive toward sin. The flesh and the world are two allies of the enemy that work for him even when he is far away from us. He keeps an eye on us particularly when we feel safe; he is always ready to launch his sudden attacks, taking advantage of the occasions when we are tired and not paying attention.

Jesus warns us about foolishly singing victory over having passed a test, as if the battle were finished. Indeed, the filthy spirit does not surrender so easily. Once forced to leave a victim,

Holy Scripture warns us, "When the unclean spirit has gone out of a man, he passes through waterless places seeking rest, but he finds none. Then he says, 'I will return to my house from which I came.' And when he comes, he finds it empty, swept, and put in order. Then he goes and brings with him seven other spirits more evil than himself, and they enter and dwell there; and the last state of that man becomes worse than the first. So shall it be also with this evil generation" (Matt. 12:43–45). The moments of rest God concedes to us are moments of grace for strengthening us even more, so that the new tests will find us stronger and more determined.

Nevertheless, it is of fundamental importance to hold before the eyes of our mind that temptation has a predetermined time. One of Satan's most effective tactics is to induce us to discouragement, engaging us in a struggle that extends over a long period of time. At times, the diabolic oppression is so intense that a person feels his energies decline at the mere thought that an attack can last even a few hours. The seducer works with great mastery on the psychological plane. We can say that it is on this level that he wins all his wars. He has the upper hand in unhinging the mind, creating fear, anguish, confusion, and discouragement. Even human wars are often fought by these means. Satan, the "murderer from the beginning," has always used psychological weapons, knowing well that they are fundamental in spiritual battles.

Satan's objective is to cause your resistance to crumble, making you throw in the towel in unconditional surrender. To achieve this, he seeks to frighten you, exaggerating his own strength as if it were impossible to resist him. Dear friend, remember that the evil one is a big inflated balloon that you can easily pop with the little, sharpened pin of your good will sustained by grace.

The evil one tries to convince you that the time of temptation will never end. Here is the subtlest of his snares. If you could resist for even a few minutes, it would be enough to suddenly dissolve the temptation. When the serpent hisses in your ear, "Sin immediately!" seeking to seize your longed-for assent, calmly respond to him, "Let's talk about it in about five minutes." If you succeed in making this decision, praying a mystery of the Holy Rosary in the meantime, the enemy, now defeated, leaves to return at another time.

The Heart of the Battle Is Free Will

Now we will enter the focal point of temptation, where victory or defeat is decided. It is very important to go straight to the crux of the problem. Otherwise, we risk the danger of raising up barricades where they are unnecessary, while leaving the most important door unprotected. By now you have before you a complete panorama of the evil one's snares, as well as some means for avoiding them and coming away from them victorious. The two great biblical scenes of the temptations of Adam and Christ have given us some incomparable teachings about this. Both scenes converge at the point of free will. All the shrewd tactics of the demon are there to obtain your assent to whatever he offers you, while all the means of grace that God puts at your disposal are there to oppose the demon with a neat refusal.

Thus the heart of the battle is your will. It is on this aspect that you must concentrate, without diverting to any other objective. Victory over the demon arises from your yes or your no. It depends, as you see, in the final instant on you alone, because even the grace that is necessary to conquer the demon needs your will to operate. It is your decision, and no other, that determines the final outcome of temptation. It is you who in the end must choose the way of salvation or the way of perdition.

Perhaps you are wondering why your free will is so decisive in determining your eternal destiny. The reason is simple, luminous, and clear. In consenting to temptation, you say yes to the evil one and become his. In renouncing that which Satan presents, you demonstrate your love of God above all things, and you prove that you are His child. Therefore, victory over evil consists in a neat and decisive no to whatever the evil one offers you or pushes you to do. You must oppose and refute satanic invitation. This implies a great effort of heart that will at times cause you to sweat blood. But exactly this, and nothing else, is the narrow way that leads to salvation.

The decision of free will is a mystery. It is the same mystery of the human person in his likeness to God. You, and only you, can pronounce a yes or no with its incalculable consequences. Man, and only man, decides his eternal destiny in a dramatic relation with grace. You save yourself if, when confronted with the proposals of Satan, you say with the strength of a striking sword, "I renounce!"

You Are the Victor if You Say, "I Renounce!"

I would like to illustrate the immortal value of these extraordinary words with a page I wrote some years ago when I was commenting on the Gospel of the first Sunday of Lent:

> Defeating temptation costs blood, it cannot be denied; thus, the light of God at the moment of temptation is important. Why? To unmask the deception, allowing God to make us understand that possessing that concrete good which we think is for our good is, in fact, not for our good

and will not make us happy. We need to ask God for this light so that this particular deception will be unmasked. We must remember all the times in which we have ceded to temptation and have thought that the apparent good was a good for us. Indeed, in all the times in which we ceded to temptation, didn't a bitter taste remain in our mouths? Did we not discover that it was actually an evil for us? Having sunk our teeth into the apple, did we not discover that it was poisoned?

Think again to when we have ceded to a temptation: Did we truly have a good; were we truly happy? No, because we immediately discovered the deception. Thus, we need this spirit of wisdom to unmask the lie and to understand that what Satan had presented to us as good was, in reality, evil. At that terrible moment of temptation, in which you were sweating blood, the demon told you that you were unable to resist that "good," that sin, that thing, that sinful relationship without which you could not live. Remember that all the times you were close to sin, Satan was telling you the same thing. Then, when you listened to him, you felt unhappy.

Satan will tell you again that you cannot live if you do not do a determined thing. Remember this: at the moment when you succeed in saying no to the evil one, the temptation suddenly collapses. You will marvel that you did not renounce beforehand what had seemed to be a thing impossible to renounce. If you defeat temptation, you will think: "Why was I betraying my God for this false good?" You will notice that temptation is truly a suggestion which deflates as soon as you pronounce your no to the evil one: at that moment, suddenly, temptation evaporates and disappears.

Satan, as St. Ignatius Loyola explains, says, "Will you really be able to renounce all the things I offer you? How will you be able to renounce for your entire life? How will you be able to renounce money, sex, pleasure? How will you be able to renounce enjoying life for thirty, forty, or fifty years?" Satan presents this renunciation to you as an unbearable weight, but if you ask for God's light, you will understand the falsehood, and you will have strength from God to say no. Suddenly, all the satanic suggestions collapse, and you feel free and light. You will say to yourself, "Was that the temptation? For a bunch of lentils I would have betrayed my God? (see Gen. 25:29–34). How stupid I was!" Having defeated the temptation, that which you have renounced will be manifested as what it really is: garbage.

St. Catherine of Siena says that when you have broken the thorn of the sensitive will of your flesh, the rose of the heart's freedom remains, and the Gospel says that Jesus, at the end of temptation, was served by angels. Having defeated temptation, you become king: you have defeated the flesh, and you have self-dominion. You participate in the kingship of God and you are served by angels. You are a free man, you are the only free man, the only sovereign one, the only true king, the only emperor, the only president of the republic, the only one with the power to decide for yourself, in your heart, for good.

See how important it is to unmask the terrible deception of temptation. Temptation is nothing other than a great satanic lie that offers you its false goods and suggests that you cannot live without them. Woe to you if you enter into dialogue with Satan. You must give him a firm no and choose the Cross. You must say, "I renounce!" You must say it sweating blood, "I renounce! I renounce! I renounce!" Every time Satan presents to you his dung, covered with leaves of golden figs, you must respond to him, "What a stench!" Repeat in the depths of your heart, "I renounce, I renounce, I renounce!" These words are like a pinprick that deflates the balloon of temptation. Suddenly the satanic suggestion disappears, you are flooded with light and joy, and God embraces you with His infinite love, giving you the gift of his kingship while the angels serve you.[7]

[7] Padre Livio Fanzaga, *Vangelo Vivo* (*Ciclo B*) *Quaresima e tempo di Pasqua* (Milan: Sugarco Edizioni, 1996), 13–15.

14

The Outcome of Temptation

Temptation Is a Double-Edged Sword

In the Our Father, Jesus does not invite us to ask the celestial Father to eliminate temptation from our lives but rather not to allow us to fall into it. From the analysis of the two great biblical texts about temptation, we see that the antagonist is the demon, albeit assisted by his allies, the flesh and the world. God does not induce us in any way or for any reason to do evil. Nevertheless, He does permit temptation so that, if we cooperate with grace, the outcome of diabolical activity is glorifying to God and useful to our souls.

The outcome of temptation cannot be taken for granted. Satan knows that he is using a double-edged sword which could turn against him and provoke results opposite to those he had planned. It is exactly for this reason that the dragon prepares in depth every attack and carries it out with great strength and determination. If the attack does not reach its objective, Satan will confront a prey that is now stronger and more aware.

It is very important to understand how temptation, even though it comes from the demon, can cause very positive results for the spiritual life. In reality, temptation represents a possibility not only for the tempter, who thinks it up and carries it out, but also for God, who in His wisdom and sovereignty permits it. It is especially in temptation that the Most High manifests His wondrous omnipotence, by which He makes an absolutely unforeseen and unexpected good arise from evil. In this way, He humbles the proud seducer, using Satan's own projects to defeat him.

In temptation, the demon seeks to lead us into sin, through which he takes possession of our souls. Sin is Satan's seal on us and the sign of his dominion. In sin, man is separated from God. He loses God's grace and friendship and falls under the influence of Satan, who is the first absolute sinner. The demon and his activity cannot be understood if not connected to moral evil. On the other hand, redemption cannot be understood except as liberation from sin and from the one who, through it, appropriates our souls. Satan tempts us to make us sin, and through the evil committed, he procures for us eternal ruin in his kingdom of death.

God, on the contrary, in permitting temptation and sustaining us in it with the help of His grace, proposes to sift our hearts, bringing to light our most hidden thoughts so that we know ourselves better. Temptation offers us the possibility of purifying ourselves in the struggle, rooting ourselves more strongly in the good, and acquiring merits for eternal life. We would have reason to complain to God if temptation were superior to our strength and if He had not granted to us the weapons with which to fight and conquer. He offers us ample possibilities of victory, and we must know how to be grateful even for temptations, persecutions, and trials—in general, for everything Satan brings against us. All of these things can be turned to our advantage, if we so desire.

Every Victory Makes Us Stronger

The final end of temptation can result in either victory or defeat. If you fall at the moment of the test, you become weaker than before. If you come out victorious, you are certainly stronger in the good and more motivated in pursuing the spiritual path. I would like you to understand how extraordinary is the victory over the evil one who tempts you to do evil. Nothing in life is more important than this. What is the point of accomplishing victory in the world, conquering it completely, crushing every adversary, if you lose your soul in the only competition that counts? You may be defeated in every war of this world, in which men fight with great ferocity, but if you have won the good fight, then you are the king.

Why are you depressed if others are richer, more respected, and more in the forefront of society? If you have God and His grace, you are the richest. Whoever has God has everything. Whoever belongs to God reigns with Him. Do not grieve if you find yourself in the margins of the world or if you are curled up under the table of the rich man to fight with the dogs for the crumbs. If your soul is filled with grace, no one is higher than you. One could be the owner of the world, but what use would it be to him if his soul were enslaved to the demon?

Victory over temptation is an event of infinite grandeur, over which there is great rejoicing in Heaven. Perhaps you do not know how to fully appreciate the grace you have received and you have not been grateful. If you had obtained the miracle of healing, you would have certainly thrown a huge party. Victory over the evil one crowns you with glory and honor, making you a partaker in the kingship of Christ. Mary and the angels admire you, as no man on earth would do.

The victorious outcome of spiritual warfare assumes an even greater value if it comes after a long series of temptations to which you have succumbed. When we have foolishly let ourselves be dominated by a mechanism of vice and have contracted sinful habits, it is not easy to break with one blow the chains that bind us to Satan. The habit of sin weakens the will and renders us slaves to sin (John 8:34). We must struggle to master ourselves and to regain the freedom of God's children. It is a struggle in which you will often vacillate and perhaps even fall, though you constantly cry out to God for help from the depths of your heart.

When you are defeated because of weakness, having fought with all your good will, immediately present a humble and contrite heart to the Lord, begging Him for the grace of victory. Every time you resume spiritual warfare, your free will gradually becomes strengthened by grace until you obtain the first victories, even though they are still fragile and uncertain. Dear friend, these initial victories have a particular value, because they are like the spring buds which bring the hope of miraculous flowering in holiness.

Every success prepares the way for others. If you come out the vanquisher in the struggle against the evil one, you will find yourself much stronger. However, do not forget that Christ's grace is the source of your vigor. If you fall into presumption, the demon will have already taken his revenge. Be thankful with sincere sentiments of gratitude and humility. In this way, God will concede to you other graces with which you will be able to advance always with more success on the spiritual road.

Every Defeat Makes Us Weaker

Do not underestimate the sins you commit. They always render you weaker and lead you deeper into the evil one's enslavement. Evil damages the ones who commits it. Evil is not committed without consequences. You were deceived into believing that you enjoyed advantages in sinning, but in reality, you have only damaged yourself. Even when we believe that we are inflicting evil on others, it always falls back on us. Dear friend, in His mercy, God has desired that those who do evil suffer the consequences. In this way, it is possible for us to unmask the diabolical deception that presents evil as if it were good for us.

Perhaps you will comprehend better if we descend to a level that is more easily understood. If you were fighting an illness or were the victim of a grave accident, don't you think that your body would resent it? There is no doubt that in the most grave situations, the consequences would be felt for an indefinite time, and you would carry the weaknesses with you your whole life. Even in the eventuality of a complete recovery, the illnesses and the injuries of the past are always there to remind us of our fragility.

Woe to him who thinks he can fool around with sin. Its poison is lethal and deeply injures the spiritual fiber of a person. One mortal sin is enough to kill our souls. What was once the temple of God now becomes the den of the infernal thief. Even after sacramental absolution, there remains a weakness which you will be able to eliminate only by fidelity to the spiritual way. Certainly, the power of grace brings about the miracle of the rebirth of the person, but it takes time and the total cooperation of a good will for the devastation of evil to be eradicated.

Victorious in temptation, Satan appropriates your soul. This happens every time you lose sanctifying grace by committing a grave sin. You have good reason to cry when you become aware, as did our first parents in the earthly paradise, that you are miserable and naked. You were deceived into thinking that you were acquiring happiness, but now you find yourself desperate. Justifiably, you feel unfaithful, untrustworthy, and dirty. You have lost your self-esteem, and even though you appear to be proud and impudent, internally you are in despair, and you hate yourself.

The greatest catastrophe that can happen to a person is to fall from the grace of God into temptation. It is a calamity far greater than the loss of life itself. This explains why St. Dominic Savio, as a boy of only fifteen, did not hesitate to affirm: "Death, but not sin!" In fact, it is better to die in the grace of God than to continue living as the evil one's slave. It is this insight that sustained the martyrs, who preferred to die rather than to renounce the Faith. Have we not received an extraordinary example in St. Maria Goretti, a girl not even twelve years old?

Do you call this fanaticism or, perhaps, just an exaggeration? No, dear friend, it is simply a lucid understanding in the light of grace of what an incommensurable evil grave sin is. Underestimation is a trap of the shrewd serpent. It is enough for you to consider the consequences of just one true mortal sin which, beyond grave matter, is committed with full awareness and total consent. This "results in the loss of charity and the privation of sanctifying grace, that is, of the state of grace. If it is not redeemed by repentance and God's forgiveness, it causes exclusion from Christ's kingdom and the eternal death of hell" (CCC 1861).

Also, the falling into sin again for a person who is already in a state of mortal sin comports very negative consequences. When sin is added to sin, the conscience is darkened until it is finally suffocated, while the chains of slavery are strengthened and the heart is hardened, rendering it ever more impermeable to the grace of conversion. There are some people who desire to touch the bottom, as if evil had a bottom. Hell is a bottomless pit, and the desire to be immersed in the depths of Satan means crossing the threshold of final impenitence and eternal perdition (Rev. 2:24).

This is the reason the demon wishes to push us further downward, multiplying temptations. He knows that every sin weakens us and drags us ever deeper into the enslavement of his kingdom of darkness. The deeper he drags us down, the more difficult it will be to ascend. The heavier and more numerous the chains, the harder it will be to break them. The further we descend into the abyss of perversion, the more certain will be his hope of dominating you forever.

The Trap of Discouragement

Falling into temptation by committing serious sin is a spiritual catastrophe, but it is not a situation with no way out. This sin of man cannot even be compared to the sin of the rebellious angels. With only one mortal sin, the human being cannot immediately arrive at a radical and irrevocable rejection of God. Even if the evil deed has been committed with full awareness and deliberate consent, God immediately offers the possibility of redemption. This is proven by the fact that His voice reproves us through our conscience and invites us to penitence and reparation. The match is not finished just because one evil deed has been committed. Satan immediately acts to consolidate his victory, while the merciful grace of God works for redemption.

If you find yourself in a state of grave sin or realize you have fallen, the first thing you must do for your good is to ask God for pardon from the depths of your heart. Man is fragile and only with difficulty succeeds in keeping intact the grace of baptismal innocence throughout the insidious traps of life. Although sins of maliciousness denote a very dangerous hardening of the heart in evil, sins of weakness, committed after a spiritual struggle, allow an immediate revival.

Before you receive sacramental Confession, put yourself before the Lord, ask Him for the grace of contrition, and formulate the purpose of never sinning again. The Lord accepts the prayer of a humble and penitent heart and forgives you immediately. Nevertheless, you have the obligation to go as soon as possible to the sacrament of Confession to receive absolution from the priest. The Act of Contrition recited from the heart immediately after a fall is a great grace for you and a burning defeat for Satan.

The evil one fears the penitence of the sinner. The voice of conscience that causes remorse is his great enemy. He will try in every possible way to stifle it and make you postpone the moment of contrition. He will seek first to minimize the evil you have committed, then to excuse it, suggesting several extenuating circumstances. Now he has you in his hand, but he does not want you to realize it. He will tell you that all men sin, in the sense of the ancient popular proverb "A trouble shared is a trouble halved." In other words, he will seek to convince you that sinning is normal and that you do only what everyone else does, so why worry about it?

To those who have a more sensitive conscience and who feel the weight of their faults, he presents other arguments. The shrewd serpent hisses in your ears words such as these: "Why not give yourself peace? You have basically fought and done everything possible for you to do. Know that man is too weak and that evil is so strong. It is impossible not to sin!" From one side, Satan succeeds in excusing in this way the sin you have committed, while from another side, he disarms you for the future, making evil appear to you as an inevitable condemnation that harms every man.

After the defeat, the demon desires your surrender. Discouragement is his secret weapon. He cannot sleep soundly while the voice of God is still resounding in your conscience. He seeks to enwrap you in total darkness, preventing grace from filtering into the obscurity of your soul. His recurring argument is that you will never succeed in breaking the chains of sin and should therefore simply surrender. After the first crippling blow, he will seek to finish you, dragging you into the abyss of abjection until any resurrection is excluded. He wishes to lead you as soon as possible to the edge of that pit from which it is difficult to emerge. He wants you to throw in the towel once and for all and to consent to eternal perdition.

Even if you have come to the edge of that abyss, and even if you have fallen into it, know that salvation is still possible. The Blood of Christ is still given to you for the remission of your sins, and the prayers of your Mother Mary, the saints, and the whole Church go up to the Heart of the Merciful One. No matter how many sins a person commits, if he does not surrender to evil but sincerely asks forgiveness, God saves him.

15

Temptation and the Capital Vices

The Allies of Satan

The satanic activity of temptation aims to entice us to commit evil, especially those who are rooted in the good. The more a person has advanced in the way of sanctity, the more he is surrounded by the demon's snares. The two great temptations that open both the Old and New Testaments are aimed at persons whose human natures are unimpaired and immune from any sin. Satan did not retreat from attacking either our first parents, constituted in grace and friendship with God, or Jesus Christ, whose humanity is the fountain of grace itself. The success the evil one had in the Garden of Eden demonstrates that his power of seduction cannot be underestimated. The infernal serpent obtained the victory alone, without those allies on which he can depend in temptations against us.

Our existential situation is one of greater weakness, even though it must not be forgotten that we are offered the overabundant grace of Christ, with which every victory is possible. After Original Sin, our nature was injured. Even after man receives the gift of sanctifying grace in Baptism, there remains in him an inclination toward evil that is not sin in itself but, nevertheless, is an inclination toward it. "Baptism, by imparting the life of Christ's grace, erases original sin and turns a man back toward God, but the consequences for nature, weakened and inclined to evil, persist in man and summon him to spiritual battle" (CCC 405).

Beyond this weakness, which is innate in our flesh and on which the demon relies heavily, Satan has another potential ally in the world in which we live. It is necessary here to make some distinctions. Undoubtedly, there is a world that is a friend of God and that helps men on the good way. We think of healthy families, good people, and certain laws and institutions that reflect the morality of God's law. We think above all of the Church, which is not of this world but is, nevertheless, inserted in it and represents an impregnable fortress and a holy pasture in which we find protection and refuge.

Nevertheless, there is another world of darkness, error, immorality, and evil, whose lord is the evil one. Today, this world influences culture, institutions, and social structures, infiltrating many different environments. It conditions the way people think, and it damages consciences. Satan's presence is so strong that even in countries with a Christian background, believers must walk against the tide, being constantly vigilant to preserve their faith and morals. His power to seduce, which is experienced particularly through the mass media, is extraordinarily incisive. At times, it leaves the impression that evil wields such a vast means of power that it is able to condition the thoughts and behavior of men, including Christians.

Nevertheless, the world would not have such great power to induce us to evil if it did not find in us well-rooted complicities. Because the public is inclined toward lust, a certain type of television commercial thrives. If there are many wars, it is because violence is itself rooted in the hearts of many. Governments approve norms that are contrary to matrimony founded on the laws of nature because men are abandoned to their passions. The corruption of society is a mirror of the corruption of the soul. It is certainly true that an immoral society induces its members to great depravation, and it is right to fight against it; but the original root is the diseased heart of man. It is there that Satan finds the support that allows his work as seducer to proceed. The seven capital vices that pollute and weaken human nature are the faithful allies of the evil one when he attempts to induce us toward evil.

Satan Acts on Our Sinful Tendencies

What are the seven capital vices? They are the sinful tendencies of our human nature after Original Sin. They are latent in us like seeds of evil that are developed step by step as we nourish and cultivate them. Their root is the selfish ego that strives to promote itself against God and against neighbor. If our good will, sustained by grace, does not fight these sinful tendencies over time and seek to uproot them, they will take possession of our being and of our lives, orienting us toward evil.

Spiritual tradition has singled out seven capital vices. Each of them is the origin of many others. They are pride, avarice, lust, anger, gluttony, envy, and sloth. It should be clear that the vices of man are much more numerous, but they can all be retraced to these seven fundamental tendencies, whose common root is the insatiable hunger for the things of the world.

There is no man who does not carry this burden of concupiscence. Even the saints did not become such because they lacked these evil inclinations but because they knew to fight them vigorously. Men are good or evil in the measure in which they engage themselves in this harsh battle against themselves. Every heart of man is like a garden where seeds of both good and evil are spread. Do not be deceived by external appearances. Whoever has not made the effort to uproot the evil weeds is like an abandoned garden that becomes a lair of serpents and scorpions.

Satan has a formidable ally in our wounded human nature. Temptation exercises such a strong attraction on us because it appeals to the evil tendencies that live in us. The more strongly they are rooted, the more difficult it will be to fight them. The more you satisfy your passions and strengthen them with sin, the easier it will be for the evil one to lure you and to make you fall. However, a mortified man, who has fought against the vices by practicing their contrary virtues, will find it easier to obtain victory. Nevertheless, no one can have any illusions of safety, not even the saints, because Adam succumbed to temptation while his nature was still intact.

Perhaps you are wondering if all these tendencies toward evil are present in every man. The seeds of these wicked weeds are found in all men, without exception. However, their development is different and depends on personal character, education, and life circumstances. Thus, it happens that while all of these ramifications of evil are present in a wounded heart, one or more of them has the upper hand over the others.

Just as there are always some trees that stand out among the others in a forest, there is one passion that emerges as the dominant one. There are some people who easily cede to the urges of sex, while others are obsessed with money, or are drawn to smoking or alcohol, or are slaves of games. Some love to speak untruthfully, to slander, and to defame; others are on an insatiable search for occasions to make themselves prominent or to be noticed. Some people are wrathful and argumentative, others jealous and invidious. In every one of us, some passions are stronger and become much more vigorous in proportion to the occasions in which we cede to their attraction.

The tempter studies each of us carefully from the time we reach the age of reason. He singles out our fundamental passions and our weaknesses. He seeks to understand to which of the capital vices we are more prone to surrender, and he attacks us from that side. We can see here with clarity the importance for all of us to know ourselves, at least as well as the demon knows us. For this reason, we must pay particular attention to the weakest parts of our nature and ward off temptations, exercising the virtues contrary to our predominant passions. If one knows he is easily excited to anger, he needs to exercise patience. If one is inclined to pride, he needs to exercise humility, accepting the humiliations of life graciously. Every opening of our souls through which the enemy could pass must be defended by the practice of virtue.

Satan Enchains Us with the Seven Capital Vices

The tradition of the spiritual masters often speaks of the chains by which the demon holds us prisoners after having pushed us to sin. What chains are these? They are none other than our vices, by which Satan tightly holds us in his hand and brings us wherever he desires. It is Jesus Himself who warns us when He says that the one who commits sin is a slave of sin (John 8:34).

These affirmations unmask the great lie spread in our times, that sin is an exercise of our individual freedom. For example, let us think about the claim to sexual freedom, which has now broken all barriers and which purports to be the way that finally leads man to self-realization and to the acquisition of happiness. It is presented as a great conquest of freedom, in which man has finally succeeded in giving meaning to his life. In reality, lust is a vice as ancient as Adam that degrades and brutalizes man through shameful practices, pollutes and destroys the chaste love of families, and coarsens and demoralizes young people while stealing dignity and serenity from older people.

The same can be said about all vice. Satan is always behind sin. Through vice, the slimy serpent enwraps us in his coils of death. In this way, he enters and takes possession of us. When the evil one disturbs the mind, the body, or even societies, as is well known to exorcists, his presence is certainly disquieting, but it is not necessarily dangerous. Quite different and much more serious is the situation in which the serpent creeps in through the passions that enslave us.

Our spiritual tradition has done an in-depth analysis of this problem. It is not only the tempter who renders us his slaves through the seven capital vices, but every vice is also presided over by a specific demon. Origen, the great Alexandrian theologian of the third century, taught that every one of the seven capital sins, together with all of its derivations, is governed by a particular evil spirit that creeps into us every time it succeeds in enticing us to sin. The more an evil habit is hardened through sin, the more the demon corresponding to that evil possesses us.

It is interesting to observe that this doctrine is revived today in groups that practice the prayer of deliverance. It cannot be denied that the practice has some roots in the patristic tradition and even in some passages of the Gospels. The case of St. Mary Magdalene, from whom Jesus cast out seven demons, can be cited here. Since Mary Magdalene was a sinner, it is evident that these demons were the demons of the seven capital vices (Luke 8:2). Even more significant is the passage in the Gospel that mentions an impure spirit who, exiting from the man, returns to find the house empty, swept, and adorned: "Then he goes and brings with him seven other spirits more evil than himself, and they enter and dwell there; and the last state of that man becomes worse than the first" (Matt. 12:45).

Whatever you may think of this specific doctrine, the rudimentary affirmation appears absolutely solid and irrefutable. Satan enchains us through the seven capital vices, rendering us slaves in his kingdom of darkness. The most terrifying diabolical possession is that which is realized through becoming familiarized with sin. The more one sins, the more the image of the evil one lives in him. Deliverance from this slavery is the greatest of miracles.

The Exorcism of Mortification

Today, the practice of exorcism is making a comeback in the Church. It will certainly receive a significant impulse with the publication of the new Ritual. It is an ancient tradition that stems from Jesus Himself and whose rebirth should be greeted as a positive fact. There is, however, the danger that the faithful think a benediction or an exorcism is enough to drive out the demon. Many are ready to see evidence of his annoying activity in sickness, psychological disturbance, disgrace, the negative events of life, and so forth.

They are less inclined to grasp the presence of the evil spirit in their own persons when they are abandoned to sin. A parent may be worried if a baby, perchance, has received a curse and will consequently rush the child to an exorcist. If no exorcist is to be found, the child may even be taken to a magician, but the parent is often far less concerned about educating the baby in the practice of good and in the life of grace.

It is incredible that so many people are disposed to see the demon everywhere except where he is most certainly present: in sin. They are few who realize that with one mortal sin, they put themselves in Satan's hands, though perhaps it would be more exact to say in his jaws, since the Scriptures compare him to a lion and to a dragon. Priests are called to bless homes thought to be possessed by malignant spirits, but at the same time, the demon has silently transformed our hearts into a den of thieves where he dwells in comfort.

The struggle against the demon is achieved primarily in the struggle against sin. Inasmuch as it regards that particular type of diabolical possession actuated through the capital vices, there is no doubt that the most efficacious exorcism is mortification. Naturally, mortification must be preceded by the sacrament of Confession, which reestablishes the soul in the splendor of sanctifying grace, and it must be sustained in the vigor of prayer, in particular, the prayers of Holy Mass and the Rosary.

Nevertheless, dear friend, do not think that the demons can be driven away from you without the mortification of those passions on which they breathe and through which they enter into you, taking possession of your soul. In its literal meaning, the word *mortification* means, "to put to death." It is not just a superficial trimming but rather an uprooting of our tendencies toward evil. All of this requires a constant and prolonged effort of the heart, often continued over time, because we do not even suspect how much work, commitment, and good will is required in the heart's purification.

Perhaps we have forgotten today the great lesson the desert fathers have given us from their daily struggles against Satan. They teach us to face the demon with the weapons of renunciation, asceticism, and continuous prayer. Inasmuch as the principal ally of Satan, the flesh, is alive and well, we are in grave danger. At times, we are deceived into thinking that we have overcome the flesh, but then we realize that "the beast" in us was only lulled to sleep. A mere pinch will not be enough to weaken it. This struggle is the most tremendous one of all, but victory is possible with grace and perseverance.

If you have defeated the flesh, you have succeeded in depriving the evil one of his most efficacious support. To arrive at Heaven, the saints had to go the way of Calvary. Today, we need to learn this lesson. We try to fight the devil with holy water, without abandoning a life of sin and turning to the way of sanctity. There is an exorcism available to everyone, and it needs no special permission to be used. It is the holy life of the children of God, which keeps the demon far away as the sun keeps darkness away.

16

Temptation in Daily Life

You have become aware that temptation is a fundamental aspect of life here on Earth. It represents a critical moment of spiritual warfare and constitutes the greatest snare for our souls and for our eternal destiny. The craftsman of this masterpiece of falsity and iniquity is the rebellious angel, assisted by his followers, whose intelligence, shrewdness, hatred, and perfidy are often neglected. When temptation is manifested, and you are aware of the snare, you are already in great danger, because the shrewd seducer has already silently enwrapped you in his net. If you carelessly enter the trap of temptation, engaging in dialogue with it rather than severing it with a neat cut, only a miracle of grace will allow you to come out of it unscathed.

Satan is particularly dangerous because he sets his traps and camouflages them perfectly among the folds of daily life. He works like termites that devour wood from the inside until the beam, which appears perfectly intact externally, suddenly collapses. He is hidden behind little infidelities, seemingly innocuous hesitations, trivial imperfections, and violations against the law of God which, at first glance, seem irrelevant. A tiny crack is enough for him to penetrate and provoke irreparable devastation. Therefore, it is useful to offer an overview, necessarily incomplete, of the openings we carelessly leave at the disposal of the evil one and through which he readily creeps without our even realizing.

The Neglect of God and Prayer

Satan attacks you from the moment you wake up in the morning, seeking first to occupy the thoughts of your mind so that God remains out of your life from the very beginning of the day. The devil attacks you with a long list of preoccupations, anxieties, and fears that crowd around you at the moment of rising. If you are not ready to find God in prayer, committing to Him your day and everything that presses on your heart, then you risk extinguishing the internal lamp necessary for your guidance and for that peace of heart that allows you to do your tasks with calmness and profit.

Satan seeks to disarm you before every temptation. He does this by taking away from you the only instrument that enables you to defeat him: prayer. In prayer, you obtain from God the light of discernment to discover Satan's snares and the strength to oppose his allurements. He will be untiring in his attempt to rob you of your daily moments for prayer, making excuses that there are other, more urgent things to do. He will seek to render your prayers insignificant or inconclusive. Once there is no more room for daily prayer, God inevitably disappears from your life. Other things have taken His place, and Satan is in a position to seduce you at his pleasure.

If the day is not illuminated and warmed by prayer, then you are at the mercy of the seducer, who will do with you as he wishes. Think about our first parents in the earthly paradise. If they had been recollected in prayer, the shrewd serpent would not have had any opportunity for victory. Jesus teaches us how to be prepared for the attacks of the evil one, recollected in the deepest union with God. The desert fathers and the saints were vigilant and prayed without ceasing so as not to fall into temptation. It is a fundamental law of Christian life on this earth, where the enemy does not sleep, that we should always be alert and prepared to repel his attacks.

Attachment to Material Things

Material things are used by Satan to oust God from your heart. The demon knows that we need temporal bread, and he shrewdly seeks to expand this requirement to make us forget our spiritual food, without which the soul cannot live. A popular Italian saying wisely refers to money as "dung of the demon." Jesus Himself sees in the love of money an insidious enemy of God: "You cannot serve God and mammon" (Matt. 6:24), a remark that allows no reply.

There are some people who put their work and profession first. Others, who live for their work, are ready to give up the time meant for their families, for prayer, and for tending to themselves just to advance in their careers. Many are ready to sacrifice the day of the Lord to earn a little bit more. Through attachment to material things, Satan causes arguments within families and among relatives. Wars themselves always originate in an interest of a material character, resulting in tremendous slaughter.

If a person is attached to money, Satan can use him for any crime. Did he not convince Judas to sell the Master for thirty pieces of silver? Woe to the one who does not know how to say no to money whenever justice and dignity require it! Consider the danger of eternal perdition that accompanies the death of one who has dedicated his life to the accumulation of riches, without any thought of enriching himself before God with the merits of good deeds. The demon leads the lover of wealth to the threshold of eternity with a heart attached to false treasures that will desert him, while faith in God and the hope of eternal life are extinguished in his soul.

With the material things he offers you, Satan steals you away from God and from Paradise. With an unattached and trusting heart, you would have daily received everything necessary from the providence of the celestial Father.

Thoughts, Worries, and the Anxieties of Life

The enemy is envious of the peace and joy God gives us, and he tries to deprive us of them. Because he does not always succeed in dragging us into sin, he seeks to work on us at a psychological level to create disquiet and anxiety. Satan exerts himself to darken our trust in the Creator, in His omnipotence, and in His providence. He causes us to become obsessed about our immediate future, making us anxious about work, home, family, health, and everything that is out of our control. He overwhelms us with distressing thoughts about things that will never happen.

Jesus warns us about this strategy of the tempter, whose objective is to make us forget that we are constantly protected by a good Father who feeds the birds of the air and clothes the lilies of the field. The divine Master gives us the day we are now living as a measure of our existence, and we must trust the Omnipotent One to give us the future with His hands full of tenderness.

The representation of the future as full of anxieties is one of the most recurring satanic tactics, and the devil uses it especially to overcome good people. At the same time, Satan seeks to reinforce evil so that those whom he has ensnared continue to move at ease along the path of perdition. If you let yourself be dominated by disturbing thoughts of fear, Satan will succeed in taking away your serenity and peace. Know that he is a master at exaggerating things so that he can agitate you even with trifles. The perfidious adversary will never overlook an occasion to oppress you with anxieties and terrors of various kinds. If you let yourself be caught in his snares, you will exhaust both mind and body, and he will take away your peace and your joy of living. To escape from this snare, you must live in the present time the Father gives you, seeking to fulfill His will moment to moment and entrusting your future to Him, because all things are in His hands, and nothing happens without His desiring it or permitting it.

Never doubt the goodness, providence, and omnipotence of the Most High. In fact, as St. Thomas Aquinas noted, the will of God is always realized. Therefore, do good and witness the love that God gives you during the day, entrusting to him all the worries, anxieties, and fears with which Satan wishes to bring you down. How many times the evil one succeeds in disturbing and frightening us with what exists only in our imagination and will never happen in the future! In this way, he has obtained his objective, taking away from us the serene tranquility of soul.

Distrust, Complaining, and Blasphemy

Although Satan lays traps for us along the road of our life, God sustains us with His grace and allows us to undergo different kinds of trials to strengthen and purify us. We do not always understand this divine pedagogy, and most of the time, we are unable to see any authentic graces in the crosses and tribulations that punctuate human life here on earth.

This is evident particularly in the moment of sickness, which, although rooted in fallen human nature, is always governed by the wisdom and sovereign hand of the Creator. In the moment of affliction, the evil one readily intervenes to take away from you the merit you can achieve through your endurance. First, he will seek to seize your confidence in God, insinuating to you that the suffering you are enduring is neither just nor paternal. This goal obtained, he will push you to complain and he will feed your heart with poison, as if God were no longer a father to you but rather a cruel stepfather.

In this way, you are closed to God, before whom you harbor a growing resentment that is slowly transformed into rage and, often, into blasphemy and cursing. You realize that the shrewd serpent has crept into your heart and made you feel his own negative sentiments toward the Creator. What should have been an event of grace (for such is always God's intention in bringing us to a test—suffering, economic reversal, tribulation, injustice, or humiliation) becomes an occasion of agitation, moral lapse, and separation from the good and merciful Father.

How different the outcome would have been if you had immediately noticed the diabolical snare and if you had submitted yourself in total trust to the will of your Lord. He would have helped you carry your cross, whatever it may have been, making it lighter and transforming it into an occasion of merit and spiritual growth.

Irritability, Misunderstanding, and Lack of Reciprocal Acceptance

The devil, as the name itself indicates, is par excellence the one who divides. While God is love and has given men the commandment to love one another as He loves them, Satan is hatred and seeks to divide men from one another and incite them against one another. He takes advantage of every occasion to create divisions, misunderstandings, fights, and arguments until he finally brings groups, peoples, and nations to the point of violence and war.

The satanic activity to create divisions is concentrated particularly on the family. The objective of the envious serpent is to separate that which God has united, especially spousal relations and the relations between parents and children, which are no less profound. This has been evident since the temptation of Eden, when the evil one disrupted the harmony of the first couple and caused our first parents to accuse one another. One of the consequences of the original Fall is the difficulty in the relationship between man and woman, who seek dominion over one another rather than reciprocal submission in mutual love.

The breakdown of the couple's relationship begins insensibly, without the spouses' awareness. Dialogue ceases and is displaced by work and the many household chores. An initial irritability appears, followed by lack of reciprocal respect. Love is taken for granted when it really needs daily manifestations of affection, tenderness, and attention. The destruction of the harmony of couples has been the foremost activity of Satan and one in which he achieves impressive results.

After the initial wearing down, the evil one moves on to the breakdown of daily dialogue, reciprocal accusations, and the erosion of trust, followed by lies, misunderstandings, and a refusal to forgive. Neither of the two spouses wishes to make the first step toward the other, and in this way, the family becomes a brood of vipers, and the children are the ones who suffer the most.

At this point, when the situation appears compromised, many couples seek the assistance of a psychologist, but most of the time, this is the first step toward separation. In fact, the psychologist is soon replaced by the lawyer, and later by the judge. The children are contested and used like merchandise for blackmail and exchange. The family is destroyed, and upon the broken pieces, the evil one builds sinful relationships which have nothing to do with the plan of God.

When the devil is unsuccessful in separating couples, he seeks at least to place the parents against the children, creating misunderstanding, lack of dialogue, and often open war. He seduces the young with the false lights of the world, driving them far away from their parents. At the same time, the parents do not have the patience of a strong and sweet witness, which would help the children escape the satanic deception and find again reasons for a sincere relationship of reciprocal affection.

Satan has sought from the beginning to strike at the most sacred relationships God has established among men, and even today he has not entirely changed his strategy. All the troubles that affect the family in the world cannot be humanly understood without the subterranean activity of the untiring serpent. The daily prayer of couples and families is the true exorcism and the greatest defense, because the struggle is not merely against flesh and blood but against the powers of evil (Eph. 6:12). Satan never tires in working to destroy the works of God, of which the family, the cell of society and the domestic church, is one of the most significant and beautiful.

Infidelity, Immodesty, and Lust

The other weapon with which the evil one ensnares the family is lust. The demon rarely limits himself to causing disagreements and misunderstandings without, at the same time, presenting alternatives which draw one or both members of the couple to irreparable choices. His minimum objective, even in the case of a couple who apparently remains united, is to stain the chaste relations of conjugal love. He circles the spouses, spying for openings through which he can enter and occasions of weakness that he can exploit.

Today, the climate that Satan has cleverly established is very supportive of so-called free love, which in reality is "vagabond love." Loyalty, sincerity, fidelity, and the transparency of conjugal love cede to the passion of mercenary and adulterous relationships in which lies, degradation, utilitarianism, and dishonesty form a toxic mixture bearing an unmistakably satanic imprint.

Lust is the capital vice that grants Satan the easiest and most lucrative successes. The incomparable deceiver has caused people to applaud as sexual freedom that leash of vice by which he leads men about like domesticated dogs. If you observe the animal world, or even the vegetable one, you will realize that sexual activity is regulated by ironclad and intelligent laws that are oriented toward a specific end. Sexual and affective disorder in man has grown to enormous dimensions. Sexuality is separated from spousal love, and in the division, both are degraded. Sexuality has been reduced to an instinct to be satisfied. The harmony and beauty of the human person, created male and female by God, becomes humiliated and scorned.

The success of the evil one here is much more visible and uncontested. Even the ones who should present the plans of God the Creator with strength and clarity have practically surrendered to this new mentality, which calls a right to freedom and to the realization of persons that which is really just a miserable and shameful slavery. The silence of many churchmen when they are faced with this satanic promotion of evil is more sorrowful and harmful than the evil itself. Satan can rejoice that today, there are no longer men like St. John the Baptist, who was ready to risk his head to denounce the sin of adultery.

Curiosity, Gossip, Lies, and Foul Language

St. Paul recommended to Timothy a fitting catalogue of widows, taking the occasion to stigmatize the comportment of some who "learn to be idlers, gadding about from house to house, and not only idlers but gossips and busybodies, saying what they should not." The apostle concludes: "For some have already strayed after Satan" (1 Tim. 5:13–15).

These observations of the apostle undoubtedly apply to everyone. We must not believe that temptation is an extraordinary event that characterizes the most important and significant moments of life. On the contrary, it is usually inserted in the very texture of daily existence, completely hidden under the guise of normality. Satan is perfectly hidden beneath an innocuous and seemingly insignificant appearance.

Let us take curiosity as an example. At first, it seems to be an innocent attitude. However, if Eve had not been curious, humanity would not have fallen into its original catastrophe. Curiosity is a desire to gain knowledge of things to which you have no right and which, in any case, are not useful to you. It is a form of spiritual gluttony that in itself is exposed to the subtle trickery of the evil one. Furthermore, it is a sin against charity, because it damages the rights of persons to privacy.

Through the curiosity of women as well as of men, the evil one profits very much. Some lose their faith because they have not known how to renounce a certain conversation. Others socialize with people whom the evil one had placed in their paths with the specific purpose of influencing them toward evil. Wishing to meddle in the lives of others, many are exposed to the danger of criticism, of gossip, and of defamation. Curious people are like hens that rummage through garbage dumps. Sooner or later, they will find a serpent that will bite them.

Look at the Virgin Mary and note with what reserve, silence, and discretion she kept the designs of God, meditating on them in her heart. Think about her visit to her cousin Elizabeth that allowed the two women to express some of the highest invocations of our faith. Base your daily life on recollection and on conversation with God. I am not telling you to be unconcerned with what happens in the world but rather to get hold of that which is truly useful and worthy of being brought to God in prayer.

Curiosity is a desire to know things that pertain to others. But why do we seek this knowledge? Maybe to pray for and help these people? Or do we only want to obtain material for gossip, expressing unjust judgments and often speaking badly about people? A proverb affirms that the tongue kills more than the sword. Think, therefore, about the crimes against charity that are committed by the tongue. With the tongue especially, Satan has caused the greatest evils against humanity, condemning many souls. As James the apostle observes, "So the tongue is a little member and boasts of great things. How great a forest is set ablaze by a small fire! And the tongue is a fire. The tongue is an unrighteous world among our members, staining the whole body, setting on fire the cycle of nature, and set on fire by hell" (James 3:5–6).

Think about the little lies, big deceptions, wickedness, insinuations, and gossip that are spread with the tongue throughout the course of our day. The hissing of the serpent comes out of our mouths instead of the praise and blessing of God. At times, our language moves from being false and poisonous to torpid and shameful, manifesting externally and before everyone the mud deposited at the bottom of our hearts. Foul language, like lying, violent, defaming, and blasphemous speech, is the sign that the demon has crept into us and gives us something of himself so that we show it to others.

Custody of the tongue, silence, recollection, continuous dialogue with God, and the gift of true and good words to our brothers are the armor with which we prevent the slimy serpent from polluting our day.

Deception, Injustice, and Dishonesty

The sphere of work, profession, and human activity in general, which absorbs a large part of men's lives, is closely studied by the tempter. We can say that the sixth and seventh commandments are the most disregarded by men, and it is here that Satan reaps his most copious harvests.

Moral theft does not always coincide with legal theft. Immorality in this field is much more extensive than illegality. How many times substantial justice is offended, even though the legal requirements are fulfilled! Satan takes advantage of our greed always to have and possess more. He pushes employers to the pursuit of ever-greater profit, disregarding the rights and needs of workers and their families. He suggests exploiting the occasions that are presented for illicit profits. He suggests not paying taxes, alleging pretexts as justifications. He pushes us to claim our rights and, at the same time, to leave aside our duties so that work loses its value as an act of solidarity and love.

When greed has grown sufficient roots, it will entice us to unrestrained theft, beginning with small things until, finally, robbery and extortion become a way of life. It is no rare thing for this to happen under the shield of law, protected by political institutions, so that even the most serious dishonesties go undetected. Under a moral profile, you cannot leave aside all the small thefts, dishonesties, and injustices that fill daily life.

Maybe the matter is not serious, but the lack of correctness shows a dishonest soul which is unstained by grave error only because of the unavailability of the occasion.

Satan, in addition to being a liar, murderer, and slanderer, is also a thief. He steals from us everything God gives us, beginning with His grace. Think about how many gifts clothed our first parents in the earthly paradise. Satan stripped them of everything, leaving them in a miserable condition. That which the demon offers us does not enrich us but rather destroys us. We can say about the things the devil offers us, using a popular proverb, that ill-gotten gains never prosper. Be on guard against his poison, seek to live honestly from your work, do your work, and be always willing to recognize what belongs to others. The celestial Father never allows the honest and loyal person to lack what is necessary.

Vanity Fair

In this necessarily incomplete overview of the many occasions in our daily lives that give an opportunity to the evil one to creep in, we cannot overlook those fed by the capital vice of pride. I would like to begin by pointing out to you the subtle poison of vainglory, which, in addition to making us annoying and ridiculous in front of others, renders even our good actions unpleasant in the eyes of God. There is a worldly vainglory which maintains that money, profession, social position, and culture are the qualifying factors of a person. Luxurious houses, elegant clothes, elaborate hairdos, and an exhibition of jewelry certainly cannot substitute for those virtues which are the true measure of a person.

Often, however, there is a vainglory that enters into the world of spiritual realities when the gifts of God are exhibited, good works are displayed, ecclesiastical offices are sought, and the cult of personality is promoted. Did Jesus not intervene, on more than one occasion, to invite those who loved to pray in public to pray instead in the secret of their own rooms or to give alms in such a way that the right hand did not know what the left hand was doing? Did Jesus not invite His disciples to take the last seats and to be the servants of all?

Satan is not humble. Being pure spirit, he certainly cannot be susceptible to the vices of men such as lust and gluttony. However, to make up for this, he is devoured by pride, which has driven him from the beginning to be hostile toward the primacy of God. He freely injects into us this poison which is his trademark, polluting even the good things we do in life. He pushes us to excel above others, to enforce our talents and strengths, to organize our lives based on the desire for worldly success, seeking always consent, approval, and applause from others. Satan exerts himself, without our awareness, to take us away from God, feeding the cult of our "selves" in the secret of our hearts.

Undoubtedly, in the worldly vanity fair, not everyone can aspire to first place. The stage, however crowded it may be, can hold only a limited number of the elect. Even if vocations are numerous, in the exclusive world of VIPs, only a few are selected. So what can we do? We seek to be first at least in our own house, in our own position at work, or within our circle of friends and acquaintances. The important thing is to find someone who will admire, revere, and serve us.

You will tell me that this is simply human weakness and not serious sin. I respond that you are either an image of Mary or of the demon. Seek to be a living image of the very humble one, who never puts herself on display and knows how to pass through the world unknown, she who is the greatest of all creatures. Work solely for love of God, love being an ordinary person, spend time with the humble and the simple, and do not be ashamed of poverty. You will then be a flower that Mary cultivates in this world of external appearances. Her scent will reawaken in the hearts of men nostalgia for being little and humble.

Jealousy, Envy, and the Refusal to Forgive

Aggressiveness and sexual disorder are certainly the more evident manifestations of Original Sin, but daily life is full of violence. I do not want to consider here the serious expressions of violence that even civil law pursues and condemns but rather those expressions of violence that penetrate the folds of daily life and through which Satan destroys fraternal love, transforming man into a wolf against his fellow man. It is incredible to witness the ease with which human beings play the part of Cain, not only through extreme forms of violence, such as murders, abortions, and wars, but also through sentiments of jealousy and envy, which provoke destructive conflicts in families, society, and even in the Church (1 Cor. 3:3).

These subtle forms of violence are no doubt very serious phenomena, even if they are hidden from public view, because they strike at the heart of relationships of reciprocal love that Christ came to bring to the earth. Surprisingly, common opinion tends to overlook the moral gravity of these phenomena, but it is a serious error in evaluation. Let us not forget that the first crime of humanity had envy as its motivation. In fact, Cain killed his brother Abel because he could not bear that Abel was better and thus more dear to God.

Jealousy and envy are evil weeds that grow everywhere, even within the sacred compounds of families and religious communities. Dear friend, think how, in the Old Testament, the brothers of Joseph were dominated by jealousy in seeing how their youngest brother was favored by God (Gen. 37:8). They unhesitatingly decided upon his death as if he were the most dangerous enemy, and only an intervention from Heaven stopped them from doing what they had proposed.

Jealousy destroys even the sacred relationship between friendship and gratitude. Consider how much King Saul owed to the courageous young man David. However, fearing that David would darken his glory, he did not hesitate to try to murder him (1 Sam. 18:8–11). Was not Jesus eliminated because of the envy the leaders of the people were nurturing against Him?

Like pride, envy is a fundamental component of the satanic poison. It is "through the devil's envy death entered the world" (Wisd. 2:24). The venomous serpent injects into us his own toxin when he succeeds in making us jealous of the gifts of others, such as when we suffer over their qualities, their successes, and even over the good that they do. If we are not ready to root out these sentiments, they will take possession of our hearts, pushing us to denigrate, defame, ill-treat, exclude, and even harm people with whom we should be united.

Jealousy and envy, even though they do not always lead to grave violence, sow discord in abundance, generating quarrels and disputes and often destroying family and neighborly relationships (see 1 John 3:14–15). People no longer speak to one another, and their hearts are closed in unforgiveness. The serpent has bitten them, and now he keeps them prisoners under the chains of resentment, rancor, and reciprocal hostility. Only the grace of forgiveness, invoked in prayer, can cause the heat of love to begin circulating and life to flower once again. The capacity to forgive without ever tiring is the most efficacious medicine against the poison Satan spreads abundantly in the affairs of daily life, attempting to make men enemies of all others.

Free Time

Free time can be well considered a gift of God. We could say that by introducing the day of rest after the six days of work, God is the author of leisure. In the divine intention, this time, free from fatigue and the concerns of life, should be dedicated not only to physical repose but also, in a special way, to the renewal of the spirit. Free time or leisure is born as sacred time that is to be dedicated to God, who is the final end of human life.

Christianity has introduced time reserved for God not only in the structure of the week but also within the day. Each day must not become a closed circle of human activity, devoted only to work, eating, and sleeping. Man's days must be opened to the breath of eternity. Prayer is placed at the beginning and end of each day so that everything begins and ends with God.

Satan works, as never before, to take over the time dedicated to God and to use it for himself. He pursues this objective, attempting to desecrate both the week and the day. He seeks to destroy Sunday as the day of the Lord to make it a day of work like the others or to render it insignificant from the spiritual point of view. At the same time, he is not at peace until he has succeeded in extinguishing from your day the lamp of prayer, which allows you to direct your steps on the good road.

The shrewd serpent has found some formidable allies, beginning with the television. In itself, it can be an instrument of good, but Satan has utilized it to destroy family prayer and to abort any dialogue between husband, wife, parents, and children. The devil has co-opted television to spread unbelief, immorality, and a frivolous and empty vision of life. In this way, the evil one has succeeded in using to his advantage that the family could otherwise use for professing the Faith, restoring the spirit, and recomposing the relations of peace.

The Deceiver

The reestablishment of family prayer, and in particular the recitation of the Holy Rosary, is certainly the most efficacious defense against the innumerable snares Satan sets today for the family, which is the fundamental rock of society and of the Church. Also, we cannot forget personal prayer, at least in the morning and at night, through which we entrust our entire day to God, ransoming it from the corruption of time and a lack of significance. When our day is under the blessing of God, the demon cannot do evil to us.

Particularly serious and even calamitous is the deception with which the shrewd enchanter has utilized the free time of young people to serve his perverse ends. Many of them pass their nights, in particular on Fridays and Saturdays, in compromising and damaging meeting places, such as bars, nightclubs, and analogous places. The slimy serpent creeps in with sex, alcohol, drugs, scurrilous language, and blasphemy, dirtying and murdering souls, poisoning hearts, and building a lair of his dark presence.

Dear young people, rediscover the light of the sun and the beauty of creation. Look at the splendor with which God has surrounded the world. The night has been made for repose and dialogue with God, Our Lady, and the angels. If you really want to stay awake through the hours of the night, begin again to contemplate the sky, the moon, and the stars, which perhaps you have not seen in years. On Sunday, instead of remaining like corpses in bed, go to Mass and then go out into nature and discover the presence of the Creator. Do not allow Satan to destroy with vice, evil, and lack of sense your life, which is a great gift of God and whose greatness and truly divine beauty you cannot imagine.

17

Temptations on the Way of Conversion

Satan Fears the Penitent

The mercy of God does not abandon the sinner. To our first parents, who had fallen into the satanic net, God promised the Redeemer and victory over the infernal serpent. The Cross of Christ has expiated all the sins of the world, and divine pardon is offered for every fault, no matter how great it may be. When a person falls into sin and loses sanctifying grace, God does not cease to concede to him graces of conversion so that he opens his eyes to the evil committed and returns to the right way.

Satan, after he has captured a soul, cannot sleep soundly. From that moment, the most difficult phase begins for him, because the soul could escape from him at any time. In fact, after the fall into sin, the satanic enchantment is broken, and the sinner experiences the disillusionment of a miserable existential condition which destroys the illusion of promised happiness. The conscience suffers remorse, and the scales fall away from the eyes. You realize that you are naked, deprived of God, His grace, and your dignity. Nostalgia for lost innocence begins to rise up from the bottom of your heart, which is not yet hardened in evil.

The crucial moment for the evil one happens when the sinner, under the prodding of grace, is conscious of the deception into which he has fallen and the danger of the evil way on which he finds himself. The first thing that the expert deceiver will seek to do is to dull the voice of conscience. Through the voice of conscience, God disapproves of what you have done and calls you to change your life. If you committed adultery, your conscience will say to you: "You have betrayed trust, you have soiled your marriage, you have put your family in danger, and perhaps even the family of your partner in sin. On this path, you risk eternal damnation."

Satan must absolutely silence this voice, so he will reply with alleged excuses and deceptions. He will seek to calm you down by telling you that no one will discover anything; there is nothing evil if there is love; these are all taboos invented by the Church; everyone does these things; Hell is empty. He will tell you that even your parish priest cites some theologians who are of this opinion. His objective is to impede, at any cost, the remorse of conscience leading to repentance and to the decision to find a priest for the reception of the sacrament of Confession.

But these lies are not enough. Satan knows that if a soul is not chained, she could fly away from him at any moment. He recognizes that it is not enough simply to hold a soul in a trap; he must not only block her escape but remove any possible hope of redemption. The shrewd serpent understands that his conquest must be consolidated, and he can only achieve this goal if the soul suffers successive falls, each of which weakens her until she has become a total slave to sin.

For this reason, the tempter goes to work again, so that the fault committed becomes a well-rooted vice and the habit of sin is formed. The objective is to bring the heart of the sinner to a love of evil and to make him arrive at a point of such perversion that he is in solidarity with evil and becomes one of Satan's collaborators. Then he is one step away from final impenitence and

Satan can count him among the secure members of his kingdom of darkness.

Repentance is Satan's great defeat. With it, the dragon loses all that he had won with great effort. With sorrow for sins and the intent never to commit them again, the soul returns to God and is saved. You can imagine with what effort the demon seeks to impede repentance and to render inefficacious all the graces God has given to call the sinner back to Himself. Along these front lines, the eternal destiny of many souls is decided. This is true not only in the course of life but also in its final moments, when a dying sinner's gaze is fixed on a crucifix or the invocation of the sweet name of Mary bears witness to the final victory of grace.

He Impedes Confession

It is not rare that grace breaches the sinful heart and causes one to consider the possibility of searching for a priest to whom he can confess. Having been unsuccessful in his attempt to suffocate repentance, the tenacious and untiring demon quickly raises up another barrier. His concrete objective is to prevent your ever making it to a confessional. He knows that if he is successful in blocking your way on the path that leads to the Church, the tiny bud of penitence will wither and die.

To obtain his end, the demon will neglect nothing. He will insinuate to you that there is no need to confess your sins before a man but rather that it is sufficient to ask pardon from God directly. Seeing, however, that you are determined to find a church, he will do everything to entice you to postpone the decision to another moment. Know that the weapon with which the demon renders many conversions useless and by which he avoids a certain defeat is that of convincing you to put off, even for a short time, your resolution of going to Confession.

Dear friend, if grace has touched your heart and you have decided to go to Confession, do it immediately and not tomorrow. Satan, when he is unsuccessful in preventing your making a decision to do what is right, will seek to convince you to postpone it. He needs only a small amount of time, even just a few hours or, sometimes, even just a few minutes, to sneak in a little doubt and cause you to backtrack. While God says, "today," the tempter says, "tomorrow," or "later," so that he succeeds in stealing from you the time allotted for conversion.

Even when the evil one sees you arrive at the confessional, know that he will not cease to thwart you. Perhaps the priest is not available at that exact moment, so the demon takes advantage of this by making you postpone Confession to an undetermined time, insinuating to you that priests are difficult to find and that they are really unwilling to hear Confessions. But what would you do in an emergency if you could not find a doctor? Would you not search for another one?

Once you are kneeling before the crucifix, in the presence of God's minister, can you feel safe? The slimy serpent is not yet vanquished and will seek to provoke in you feelings of fear and shame and concern about the opinions of others. He will attempt to make you remain silent about some serious sins, rendering the Confession invalid. Dear friend, at that moment, pour out your heart completely, fearlessly, and without holding back anything, remembering that you are not in front of a man but rather in front of Jesus Christ, who rejoices over your repentance and voluntarily takes all your sins upon Himself to destroy them in His love.

With the absolution of the priest, the satanic chains are broken, and you have once again found the freedom and joy of the children of God within the holy fold of His Church.

He Insinuates Doubts about Forgiveness

After the joy experienced in the sacrament of Confession, one enters into a period full of difficulties, but this is time that does not impede the spiritual way but rather renders it even more solid. Satan does not resign himself to lose a prey he had already considered his own, and he will do anything to take it back again. If he sees that you are determined in the way of conversion, and he does not find openings to present his ancient seductions, he will search for a means to take away your serenity and peace of heart.

Satan will begin to raise doubts about your confession, which has constituted the decisive turning point of your life. He will hiss in your ear that you may have forgotten some sin. On the other hand, after so many years of not making an examination of conscience and not confessing, how could you make a perfect presentation of the state of your soul? But an expert confessor always knows how to grasp the essentials of an interior situation and does not need to hear many words. The priest has seen your repentance and all the evil you have consigned to merciful love. At the moment of absolution, which he has given you in the name of Christ, you feel a great peace.

However, the evil one wants to steal this peace from you, and after casting doubts about your confessed sins, he makes much more serious and dangerous insinuations to you. He begins to sow the suspicion that God has not forgiven you. In Sacred Scripture, Satan is sometimes called the "accuser" (Rev. 12:10). This function he unfolds in a very subtle way when he enlarges before your eyes the sins you have committed, the sins that he himself pushed you to commit. His objective is to make you doubt God's forgiveness, as if for your particular situation there is no possibility of redemption. "Has God forgiven me?" you begin to ask yourself, distraught with an increasing sense of doubt.

If this doubt starts to creep in, you find yourself in a very insidious situation, because your confidence in Divine Mercy, the very heart of conversion, is in jeopardy. If you give into this tremendous temptation, you risk being sucked into the whirlpool of desperation, as happened to Judas. One of the most important and decisive battles begins for you. You must make a serious effort in your heart to believe that God has forgiven you. It is not easy, because the evil one will attack you with thoughts and doubts of every kind in an attempt to render your confession useless.

In the spiritual combat, repeatedly renew the acts of faith in the merciful love of Christ. Think about the words He said to the adulteress: "Neither do I condemn you; go, and do not sin again" (John 8:11). Kneeling before a crucifix, think again about the words the dying Jesus said to the penitent thief: "Truly, I say to you, today you will be with me in Paradise" (Luke 23:43). Every time the accuser insinuates doubt to you about God's forgiveness, meditate on the words the Lord Himself said to the prophet Ezekiel: "If the wicked restores the pledge, gives back what he has taken by robbery, and walk in the statutes of life, committing no iniquity ... none of the sins that he has committed shall be remembered" (Ezek. 33:15–16).

Insinuating doubts, fears, and uncertainties about the sins of your past life, Satan succeeds in taking away your peace, but above all, he weakens your faith in God and thus blocks your spiritual way. In forcing you to look back, he succeeds in entangling you in a past that God has already consumed in His divine love. In this way, Satan impedes you from fixing your gaze toward the future and walking with conviction in the road that leads you to holiness. You, like Paul, who was also a great sinner, must move ahead "forgetting what lies behind and straining forward to what lies ahead." Therefore run "toward the goal for the prize of the upward call of God in Christ Jesus" (Phil. 3:13–14).

Resistance and Perseverance

Conversion is a grace of boundless greatness, but it has an unyielding enemy in the demon. He will make every possible effort to destroy it. In this, he has a faithful ally in our flesh. Every authentic change in life requires a renunciation of sin and the mortification of those passions which lead to it. After the joy experienced in being freed from the chains of evil, the passions reawaken. Accustomed to being satisfied whenever they so desire, they do not bear well the fast imposed on them with an iron will.

If you are strongly committed to your decision and unfailingly deny the demands of the flesh every time they raise their head, you will proceed freely in the way; but if you hesitate and concede to the flesh, mortified but not yet dead, it will regain strength very quickly and knock ever more violently on the door of your heart, demanding to be satisfied. If you concede a fingernail to the demon, he will take your hand. Let the passions launch their cries of protest. The less you listen to them, the quicker they will become silent. However, if you begin to compromise, the unclean spirit that previously ruled you will return with seven spirits worse than himself, and your ruin will be decided (Matt. 12:43–45).

The assaults of the demon after you have driven him from your house will be, without any doubt, more violent and much more fierce. At first, you may be surprised, if you were of the erroneous opinion that with Confession, temptations would be diminished. But God sustains you with His grace, and He allows these furious attacks to consolidate you in virtue. In fact, no virtue is truly such without being tested (Rom. 5:3).

You can compare returning to God in Confession with cutting the grass of a meadow, to use an image dear to St. Catherine of Siena. But if you want to sow wheat in that field, you must plow deeply and eliminate the weeds at their roots. The storm of the passions after conversion and the tests through which the soul is called to pass have the aim of removing the deep roots of evil. It is a long and painful operation, but a necessary one. Whoever does not face it will return, sooner or later, to the dominion of the infernal tyrant.

Therefore you begin the time of resistance. Just as when you were wrapped in the vortex of seduction, you needed to repeat incessantly in your heart, "I renounce," now that you are on the good way and know the evil one's traps well, you must to say to yourself, "I resist." These are two expressions which, like sharpened spears, deflate the temptations and illustions of Satan and dissolve them into nothing.

Resistance and perseverance are the wings which make it possible for you to soar like an eagle through the skies of holiness. But as you follow the spiritual way, the tempter changes his tactics. He realizes perfectly that he can no longer seduce you with those things whose deception you have personally experienced. He will use other strategies, much more subtle and dangerous, to create obstacles in front of you as you travel in the good way.

From the sins of the body he will pass to the sins of the spirit. Montfort observed that many ascetics who were successful in castigating the flesh like eagles in God's sky, were then transformed into birds of the night. Satan is very capable of presenting himself under the guise of an angel of light, and it is exactly in this way that he succeeds in seducing those souls who are more open to supernatural realities.

As you see, most dear friend, the way of salvation is strongly contested. The struggle will accompany us until the final instant, and only those who persevere with good will until the end will be saved (Matt. 10:22). However, you must neither be saddened nor discouraged. In fact, in every tribulation and temptation, the heart of the Christian overflows with joy (2 Cor. 7:4). God guards and protects us and does not allow Satan to do evil to us if we do not desire it. Even all the snares of the evil one will be transformed for us into good. Mary protects us under her mantle and with her maternal presence softens even the most difficult moments. On the way of holiness, you will discover more and more the beauty and greatness of life when God's sun shines on it. I have never known anyone who repented for having persevered on the good way.

18

The Ferocity of the Dragon

Satan Seduces to Destroy

Until now, we have considered the evil one, above all, under the aspects of a tempter. With his incomparable ability to seduce, he presents himself as the one who offers to man the good he needs to be happy. This capacity of Satan to camouflage himself as a benefactor deceives many. In the common person's opinion, Satan is rarely grasped in his dangerousness and true ferocity. Only through the Scriptures and the light emanating from the life of the saints does the "mystery of iniquity" reveal its power of deception and ferocity (2 Thess. 2:7, Douay-Rheims). The horror of Hell is well described there. The wickedness of men, of which every day offers us outstanding proof, is already the reflection and anticipation of Hell on this earth.

The biblical images of the serpent, lion, and dragon complement each other in describing the evil one. The serpent is a symbol of shrewdness, while the lion and the dragon are symbols of ferocity. However, Satan cunningly wears the clothes of your life's benefactor while he seeks to destroy you through what he offers. What happened to our first parents must always be clear in your mind. Willing to accept what the tempter offered them, they lost the great benefits they had received from God and, as a consequence, brought humanity to ruin. You can verify from personal experience that, having accepted what the seducer offered you in temptation, you found yourself in a miserable condition.

The evil one never contradicts himself. He hates both God and man, as only he is able. All his proposals aim to capture us and to destroy everything good in us. In reality, what he can give us is his desolation, unhappiness, hatred, and desperation. Never expect anything positive from Satan. If you listen to his seductive voice, you will soon feel the pressing of his claws. Every time you are in need, turn to God. He is your Father, and He provides all the spiritual and material necessities to His children. While Satan destroys you with what he offers, God nourishes and edifies your life with what He gives.

He Sows Discord

Satan does not always present himself in the clothing of the seducer. There is a fundamental aspect of his activity which we will not grasp if we do not directly see his work as the sower of hatred and violence. Through the capital vices of pride, wrath, and envy, he engages in an untiring action to incite men against each other, to divide families, to create arguments and struggles in society, and finally, to provoke wars. The enormous river of blood that flows on the earth, beginning with the assassination of Abel right up until the enormous massacres of our times, demonstrates how much the poison of satanic hatred has influenced man.

There is a very instructive Gospel parable that compares the Kingdom of Heaven to a man who has sown good seeds in the field; "but while men were sleeping, his enemy came and sowed weeds among the wheat, and went away" (Matt. 13:24–25). Satan is an untiring sower of discord. We can say that he divides his time into equal parts: one part for seducing men, the other for dividing them.

Naturally, the final objective is to bring them to ruin, because his inextinguishable hatred is the catalyst of all his activity.

The sowing of discord in its many different aspects occurs mostly with the precise and indispensable help of the human tongue. With the tongue, lies are diffused, arguments are begun, and defamation and calumniation are spread, creating divisions in families and agitation and struggle in society, even, at times, in ecclesiastical communities. There is never peace where the demon is in action. If you feel a sensation of peace and serenity upon entering a home, workplace, or religious place, then God is present there, even though in a silent and hidden way. However, where there is agitation, gossip, envy, polemic, and internal struggle, know that the evil one is at work and puts one against the other by his astute direction.

One particular kind of discord the enemy spreads, especially in the field of the Church, where the good seed of God's Word is sown, is that of error. If you look back at Christian history, you will realize how many have sought to disseminate errors against faith and morals. The apostles in their time had to struggle strenuously against false prophets who looked like lambs but had the voices of dragons (Rev. 13:11). The heresies, schisms, and apostasies that incessantly injure the Church throughout the course of her pilgrimage on earth are incomprehensible without the untiring work of the devil who "is a liar and the father of lies" (John 8:44). Through lies, he has caused bloody injuries to the body of the Church, which we are called to heal with the medicine of truth and love.

He Instigates Violence

I would like to draw your attention to a very instructive affirmation addressed to the Ephesians by the apostle Paul. Among the various exhortations, there is one that is particularly striking regarding the capital vice of anger. He says: "Be angry but do not sin; do not let the sun go down on your anger, and give no opportunity to the devil" (Eph. 4:26–27). Undoubtedly, the evil one blows on the fire of all our passions, but he is particularly at ease with anger, because it is a reality that is connatural with his being, dominated by hatred. When we become impatient and anger swells within us, Satan takes advantage of the occasion to make us lose control over ourselves, pushing us to extreme actions.

Observe a man when he is angry. From his mouth come the darkest threats and most torpid blasphemies. When anger overflows from his heart, he loses any form of control and is capable of the most violent actions. Many times he is driven to murder by his blind fury. Many crimes, often perpetrated within the family home, are committed with a ferocity that cannot be humanly explained. Confronted with the many horrors of daily news reports, we conclude that people who commit such crimes must be out of their minds. In reality, there is an angle that escapes exterior observation, the presence of the one who, according to Jesus' affirmation, "was a murderer from the beginning" (John 8:44). How else can we explain the bloodcurdling sexual perversions in our times that lead to such ruthless crimes, if not by the presence of the spirit of evil in these people?

When we lose control of our emotions, we easily give in to sinful acts. Having allowed himself to be possessed by the spirit of jealousy, did Saul not attempt to murder David (1 Sam. 18:6–11)? Did Satan not enter into Judas to bring him to crime and betrayal (John 13:27)? Although in certain forms of suicide, a psychological illness can be justly supposed, in other forms, in which there is despair of God and deep darkness, the direction of the evil one can be seen. Did not the miserable end of Judas, in spite of the grace given to him of the reawakening of his conscience (Matt. 27:3), testify to the perfect satanic plan, enticing him first to homicide and then to suicide, as happens every day?

Satan provokes man to anger, and through anger, to crime, burning the soul with fury and darkening the mind, leading to the suppression of one's own life as well the lives of others. You must be vigilant and exercise dominion over yourself, controlling your tongue and forcing yourself not to act until peace has returned to your heart. Only then will you be in a condition to speak and work as you let yourself be guided by the Spirit of God (see Gal. 5:22).

He Provokes Wars

War is the organized form of violence. The root that feeds it is hatred, without which it could not be sustained. The most evident perversion of war is that the brother who should be loved is transformed into a hated enemy. Inasmuch as it is a negation of love, it is a negation of God and of His commandments. Like death, war entered the world because of sin. Immediately after the eviction from Eden, Sacred Scripture recounts that Cain murdered Abel. Violence is the first of the toxic fruits of Original Sin.

In war, Satan rallies all the vices of man. Pride, violence, theft, lust, arrogance, scorn, lies, cowardice, deception, and all possible forms of human perversion are spread abundantly among the hearts of men by the evil one. It is the time of darkness par excellence, in which Satan succeeds in conquering the greatest number of souls. In this time, all Hell breaks loose on the earth, and there would be no possibility of salvation for man if God did not illuminate the world through the burning lamps of the love of good men.

It is still discussed whether or not a just war can exist, one which is morally licit under the conditions that justify a legitimate defense. Even though a reflection of this kind has validity from the point of view of natural law, there is no doubt that the Church in the last decades has invited mankind to rise above this means of resolving controversies among groups and peoples, preferring other instruments more in conformity with the dignity of man.

The fundamental problem for the Christian lies in understanding the phenomenon of war in its true depth. In this regard, the evil one's capacity to deceive is heightened, and only discernment arising from prayer and the heart of the Church's ardent love can preserve us from erroneous judgments. In the past century, we have seen the most devastating wars in the history of humanity, with Christians on both sides, every one of them convinced of being right. In reality, only the Holy Father was right, when he spoke at the beginning of the Second World War of the "useless massacre."

In the light of the Faith, war is a satanic feat. Satan desires it with all his might, because it is his most lucrative instrument for stealing souls and bringing humanity to destruction. Wherever Satan is found, the task of the Christian is to be a bearer of peace. In the hour of darkness and hatred, the task God entrusts to the Christian is that of witnessing to the light and to love. It is in situations such as these that God abundantly concedes the grace of martyrdom to all those who believe that evil can be defeated by good.

There is no doubt that war has an infernal matrix, but its outcome is determined by the weapons of light. Christ, not Satan, governs the world and, in the final instant, the efficacious decisions are made by Christ. It is worth noting that in the revelations of Fatima, the end of the First World War depended on the recitation of the Holy Rosary, as Our Lady had asked of the little shepherds. Anyone deluding himself that men by their strength determine the course of historical events might smile at the thought. In reality, the true struggle is between light and darkness, good and evil, Christ and Satan.

This vision of faith, which grasps the roots of events and the reality of the forces that are struggling, has very important consequences for the conduct of the Christian. He, too, must be very active at the moment of the strongest manifestation of the forces of evil. His weapons will be those of the light (Rom. 13:12): first, unceasing prayer for peace and then the witness of love as he recognizes in every man a brother to defend, protect, and help. These are the weapons that influence events and determine victory, because God has the true power, while Satan and his followers have only a false strength. Christians must not be impressed nor allow themselves to be led astray by Satan's deceptive appearance of power.

He Persecutes the Church

Failing in his first attempt to seduce Christ, Satan opposed and persecuted Him, finally leading Him to the most painful and humiliating death. The Passion is, at the same time, both the greatest manifestation of hatred and the greatest manifestation of love. Satan carried out his project of eliminating Christ from the face of the earth, while Christ, responding to evil with good, accomplished the most admirable work of redemption. It is in the Passion that the evil one demonstrates the depths of his boundless and inextinguishable hatred against God and man. When he does not succeed in seduction, Satan attacks with disturbances and violence of every kind.

This is the key to interpreting the persecutions against the Church and against individual Christians. The root that feeds them is the evil one's hatred. He works untiringly to seduce the Church and to persuade her to be unfaithful to the Gospel. Of course, he is successful with some individual members, but he can do nothing against the entire building constructed on the firm rock of Peter's faith. Christ's affirmation that "the gates of Hell shall not prevail against it" does nothing but increase Satan's fury and his will to destroy the Church (Matt. 16:18, Douay-Rheims).

The apostles, who had learned from Christ to recognize the evil one's activity, are very lucid in attributing to his subtle and untiring action the oppositions and misfortunes of the apostolate. St. Paul, writing to the beloved community of Thessalonica, says that it was his eager desire to see them face to face: "Because we wanted to come to you—I, Paul, again and again—but Satan hindered us" (1 Thess. 2:18). Naturally, this hindrance will be manifested through specific occurrences or people, but Paul looks to the profound causes, discerning the work of the enemy who opposes the plans of God with all his might.

The letter from the book of Revelation to the Church at Smyrna is also very illuminating. Tests and persecutions caused by the evil one were intensified in this community: "Do not fear what you are about to suffer. Behold, the devil is about to throw some of you into prison, that you may be tested, and for ten days you will have tribulation. Be faithful unto death, and I will give you the crown of life" (Rev. 2:10). The formal act of throwing someone into prison is without doubt a human power, but the Word of God pushes us to look further and see the relentless struggle that the evil one leads against the Church until the end of time.

The entire prophecy of the book of Revelation reveals to us the impressive scenes of the bloody persecution the dragon brings against the elect until the final and definitive victory of the immaculate Lamb. Having attempted in vain to swallow the Son born of the woman, the dragon "was angry with the woman, and went off to make war on the rest of her offspring, on those who keep the commandments of God and bear testimony to Jesus" (Rev. 12:17).

The Church navigates through the sea of history among the seductions and persecutions of the great dragon. The testimony of Scripture is so strong and explicit in this regard that the desire to ignore it is an indication of that blindness which is one of the most dangerous weapons of the evil one (2 Cor. 4:4). Persecution, although painful, does not represent a danger in itself, provided that the faithful have the will to resist until death. Martyrdom may be the greatest of graces, since it assimilates us into the Passion of Christ in a perfect way. Whoever gives his life for love of the Lord is immediately assumed into Paradise, and the Church considers him a saint without requiring the test of a miracle.

Some are led to think that the witness of faith to the shedding of blood belongs merely to the first ages of Christianity. In reality, every Christian who desires to remain faithful must have the interior disposition to lose the life of his body rather than the life of his soul (Luke 12:4). When seduction does not obtain its desired effects, the great dragon unleashes the most bloody persecutions (Rev. 11:7–10). Those whom he does not succeed in seducing he hopes to weaken and defeat with trials and tribulations of every kind.

Of course, these prospects can seem excessive to our worldly and mediocre Christianity. However, from St. John the Baptist, the precursor, to Christ, the faithful witness, to the apostles, the pillars of the Church, there are none who died in their beds. The palm of martyrdom is a gift of immense grace that God gives to those whom He has prepared for a long time in the secret of their hearts. The age of martyrs has not completely come to an end, because the beast that has come up from the abyss (Rev. 11:7) is now more active than ever. Every Christian can at least aspire to that palm of martyrdom "by pin pricks," as St. Thérèse of the Child Jesus called it, by accepting and resisting those little daily persecutions that the world and the evil one unleash continually against the followers of Jesus.

19

The False Angel of Light

True and False Supernatural

A traditional saying asserts that Satan is God's ape. It is a colorful expression that grasps the substance of a statement by St. Paul: "And no wonder, for even Satan disguises himself as an angel of light" (2 Cor. 11:14). Not only does the seducer deceive, presenting evil under the form of good, but he also hides himself under the appearance of God's messenger. This theme is strongly present in Sacred Scripture, especially concerning false prophets, who come to us dressed as sheep but underneath are rapacious wolves (Matt. 7:15). In the text cited, St. Paul sees the presence of Satan, masked as an angel of light, in the "false prophets" who fraudulently claimed to be apostles of Christ.

Nevertheless, the affirmation of St. Paul is more general and deals with the problem of discernment regarding supernatural phenomena. In this sphere, the great deceiver is not afraid to imitate God, to entice men to error and draw them closer to himself. When it serves his purpose, the evil one does not hesitate to dress in religious clothes, knowing well that in that guise, he can succeed in attracting people whom he could not seduce in other ways. This leads to the very delicate problem of determining true supernatural phenomena from false ones. It is in large part a task entrusted to the ecclesiastical Magisterium; but in this field, even the faithful must refine their capacity for judgment, because the possibilities of deception today are more numerous than ever.

It is necessary to keep in mind the attitude of the Church in this matter. She does not exclude supernatural manifestations in principle. However, she approaches them with great prudence, subjecting them to an in-depth examination and evaluating the fruits of sanctity they produce over time. The works of God, even though the deceiver seeks to imitate them, have an unmistakable mark by which the prudent faithful can distinguish the true light from the false one, even in the case of phenomena about which the Church has not given a ruling.

The authentic supernatural always has a beauty, dignity, and a clear mark of evangelical simplicity. The persons through whom God chooses to communicate are characterized by humility, peace, and transparency. They are called to follow a spiritual life in the midst of the world, often carrying crosses of various kinds. They do not always become saints in the canonical sense of the term, but they have a moral integrity that renders them credible. The supernatural fruits are not necessarily manifested in a sudden and flashy way and should not be confused with the fictitious successes of false prophets, false seers, and gurus of various kinds. They provide, as their action comes into fruition, an intimate conversion that gradually matures on the tree of the Church.

The spurious supernatural is like the imitation of a painting. It seems true, but in reality, it is false. To perceive the deception, it is necessary to have a very pure heart and the gift of discernment. The Church cannot give a judgment on everything, thus the faithful must evaluate spiritual phenomena with great prudence. A cause of serious concern is the attitude of many people who, instead of building their own spiritual lives based on the Church's institutions, run here and there wherever there are rumors of supposed supernatural phenomena, exposing themselves to the real danger of being snared by the evil one and his followers.

Exterior religious signs are no guarantee. The devil can dress himself as a friar. Regrettably, we find many people and groups who deceive with messages of dubious origin, self-proclaimed seers, makeshift exorcisms, and bogus healers. At times, even priests can be deceived by these groups. The desire of people to find signs of the presence of God in human history and their own lives is certainly understandable and correct. However, this presupposes a maturity in the Faith which is not found in those people who, instead of thoroughly studying sound doctrine, run here and there with itching ears to find something that satisfies their curiosity (2 Tim. 4:3).

False Prophets

The father of lies (John 8:44) hides behind false prophets. Who are they? They are all those who seek to lead believers astray from revealed truth. The great liar has as one of his primary objectives to adulterate the Word of God and to extinguish the living flame of faith. His activity in this field is inexhaustible and began at the very beginning of evangelical preaching, as the apostle John attests: "Beloved, do not believe every spirit, but test the spirits to see whether they are of God; for many false prophets have gone out into the world" (1 John 4:1).

Today, false prophets and false teachers are so numerous that the Christian risks deforming or losing his faith if he is not vigilant and does not keep his eyes fixed on the supreme Shepherd of the Church. In a multi-religious society, in which ancient and new sects proliferate, whoever is not grounded in the truth runs the risk of being ensnared by activists and missionaries who preach the most diverse religious doctrines but who have in common an irreducible aversion to the Catholic Church.

Many of these proselytizers are outside the Christian community and are thus more easily identifiable by the faithful. The most serious danger occurs when the preaching of error happens within the Church by people who pay no attention to the teachings of the Magisterium. At times, even scholars and priests propose teachings that are ambiguous or contrary to the Faith. In this case, the damage is a lot more serious, either because of the scandal given or because of the followers they attract. In this way, Satan sows the bad seed of error and division, bringing the most fragile souls to ruin.

Today, a very subtle method, almost impalpable and invisible, is used to erode the solid foundations of the Faith. It consists in not mentioning some uncomfortable truths, those that are not believed by the world or are contested or unheeded. This obscuring of some truths of faith and morals is one of the most dangerous expedients of the shrewd serpent, because it allows many preachers and catechists to present a mutilated faith without exposing themselves to the intervention of ecclesiastical authority. Look at the silence about Hell, or about moral norms thought to be too demanding, or about the reality of sin, or about the necessity of Confession, and so on and so forth. In this way, the Faith is almost imperceptibly watered down, and Christian life loses its orientation toward sanctity as it becomes mired in mediocrity and permissive morals.

Often corresponding to this mutilation of the Faith on the level of daily catechesis in the community is a superficial and incoherent attitude of the faithful, retaining from Catholic doctrine only that which interests or pleases, leaving aside all the rest and even casually taking beliefs from other religions according to personal tastes.

Realize, dear friend, that the enemy of light works intensely against the Faith, attacking it both externally and internally with false teachers of every kind. You can see the necessity on your part of a solid religious foundation and a constant reference to the teaching of the ecclesiastical Magisterium, which has received from Christ the grace of maintaining the Church in the revealed truth.

False Spiritual Phenomena

Another sphere in which the demon disguises himself as an angel of light is that of phenomena, such as visions or apparitions. In some cases, these are recognized by the Church as deriving from supernatural origins, but the deceiver deftly imitates them to deceive simpler people and lead them away from the right road. The most frequent case is that of apparitions, which have a notable importance in the history of salvation, in both the Old and New Testaments. We cannot forget that our salvation story begins with the apparition of the angel Gabriel to the Virgin Mary and concludes with that of the Risen Christ.

Successive apparitions, throughout the history of the Church, do not constitute a part of biblical revelation but undoubtedly represent frequent interventions of God in the lives of men. Significant and numerous witnesses of the visible manifestations of Jesus and of Our Lady have been present everywhere and in every stage of the Church's history, even among serious and credible people such as the saints.

The influence these manifestations have had on the lives of believers cannot be forgotten. Let us think about some special devotions, such as the devotion of the Sacred Heart, which has taken great impulse from the apparitions of Jesus, first to St. Margaret Mary and later to St. Faustina Kowalska. Let us think of the great Marian sanctuaries, in particular those of Guadalupe, Lourdes, and Fatima, that were built on places where Mary appeared and whose continuous influence has grown in the Church and in the lives of the faithful.

Because of the positive impact these apparitions have on the reawakening of the Faith, Satan attempts to infiltrate himself to deceive, discredit, and arouse mistrust. The epidemic of visionaries (at least fifty according to historians) who hit Lourdes and its surroundings at the time of Bernadette is well-known. Even one of the eyewitnesses, the first historian of the apparitions, J. B. Estrade, upon seeing the ecstasy of one of the self-appointed seers, was taken over by enthusiasm and exclaimed: "They who do not believe are riffraff." On the contrary, he was deceived, even though he had been able to see Bernadette and hear her own testimony of the apparitions of the Immaculata.

That the evil one can manifest himself through false visions has biblical support in the Pauline affirmation which we have often cited (2 Cor. 11:14). It also has the support of eminent teachers in the discernment of spirits. Especially relevant is the witness of St. Ignatius of Loyola, who tells in his autobiography of having had, in his spiritual retreat at Manresa immediately after his conversion, a unique apparition of a luminous angel which lasted for some days. He eventually discovered that the angel was the demon.

This is the reason the Church proceeds with great prudence here, paying attention to criteria well tested by experience. Phenomena such as apparitions can be of supernatural origin, but the possibility of deception or the presence of the evil one cannot excluded. Given the impressive dimension these phenomena tend to have today, a reserved attitude and attention to the positions of ecclesiastical authorities will help the faithful to avoid following persons of dubious credibility.

Another reality which lends itself to deception and manipulation is that of interior locutions. Locutions can be of supernatural origin, as some mystical experiences of saints testify, but the phenomenon is presented in our times with such great frequency that it raises some doubts. Is it merely an autonomous creation of the psyche, or is it possible to posit the presence of the deceiver in some cases? The apparent orthodoxy of the messages is not enough for a positive judgment, because the evil one can realize his purposes by a mere drop of poison in a glass of water.

Magic and Divination

Dear friend, you are realizing that everything that glitters is not gold and that Satan, God's ape, spares no effort to deceive man. Today, the swarm of pseudo-charismatic figures, especially in the shadows of the Church, and the impotent mass of messages of allegedly heavenly origin leave one perplexed and worried. These phenomena may not always begin with the presence of the demon, but wherever there is a small opening of conscious or unconscious deception, that is enough for the shrewd serpent, who never misses an occasion to insinuate himself.

A possible infiltration of the demon can be detected also in the multiple practices of divination, in which a contact is sought with the invisible world of spirits or souls of the dead with the purpose of knowing unknown realities, in particular, those concerning future events. Regarding this, the following severe judgment of the Church is enough for you:

> All forms of *divination* are to be rejected: recourse to Satan or demons, conjuring up the dead or other practices falsely

> supposed to "unveil" the future. Consulting horoscopes, astrology, palm reading, interpretation of omens and lots, the phenomena of clairvoyance, and recourse to mediums all conceal a desire for power over time, history, and, in the last analysis, other human beings, as well as a wish to conciliate hidden powers. They contradict the honor, respect, and loving fear that we owe to God alone. (CCC 2116)

Another sphere in which the demon works, or can work, is that of healers and magicians. The voice of the Church warns you with very clear words:

> All practices of magic or sorcery, by which one attempts to tame occult powers, so as to place them at one's service and have a supernatural power over others—even if this were for the sake of restoring their heath—are gravely contrary to the virtue of religion. These practices are even more to be condemned when accompanied by the intention of harming someone, or when they have recourse to the intervention of demons. Wearing charms is also reprehensible. *Spiritism* often implies divination or magical practices; the Church for her part warns the faithful against it. Recourse to so-called traditional cures does not justify either the invocation of evil powers or the exploitation of another's credulity. (CCC 2117)

Does the Church seem too intransigent to you? She is not at all. Just remember that God is your Creator and your Savior. When you are in need, you must turn to Him. Many do not persevere because faith is extinguished in their hearts, but when true religion languishes, superstition is born, and the cult of God is supplanted by the cult of the demons.

20

"Deliver Us from Evil"

"He Saw a Great Throng; and He Had Compassion on Them"

Until now, we have shed light on some of the activities of the evil one that are particularly dangerous for our eternal destiny. Murderer, liar, false angel of light: these are the faces with which Satan attacks us in the most silent and hidden way possible. The devil's field of action is immense, and it is not easy to circumscribe him to predetermined sectors. Although it is an error to see him everywhere, it is certainly foolish to deny his presence where he works to harm numerous souls.

It is the duty of the Church's shepherds to show how dangerous Satan is, to expose the temptations by which he entices us to sin and pushes us on the way of perdition. The action of the evil one cannot be underestimated; he disturbs, oppresses, obsesses, and tortures, and he causes material, physical, psychological, and spiritual damage to the people. Today, there is a tendency to explain everything by natural causes, and the devil is not recognized even when his action is clearly pointed out by the Word of God. Some go even further, denying the very existence of Satan and the rebellious angels. It is good to drive home the point that such a denial is contrary to divine revelation and leads to a shipwreck of one's faith.

A great multitude of suffering people seek the help of priests today because they feel disturbed by the demon in various ways. Many of them notice his presence in repeated misfortunes or in mysterious illnesses that strike the body or the mind. Some, especially after they have gone to séances, magicians, and so-called healers, manifest symptoms that medical science hesitates to classify and fails to heal. These unhappy people, as a last resort, seek a minister of Christ to hear and help them. Do they have a right to help? Does the Church have any obligations to them?

Concerning this, it seems necessary to go back directly to what Jesus did and what He wanted His representatives on earth to do. The actions of Jesus and His apostles must be taken seriously. His actions contradict the affirmation of certain pseudo-exegetes, according to whom everything said in the Gospels regarding the demon and his activity can be explained by the magical thinking of the time. This position would empty of content the Redemption achieved by Christ. Indeed, it is a truth of the Faith that "by his Passion, Christ delivered us from Satan and from sin" (CCC 1708).

The Church, and priests in particular, must have the same attitude that Jesus had when faced with the suffering multitude (Matt. 14:14). He, at the end of a day of preaching, permitted the crowds to draw near to Him, bringing their miseries: "That evening, at sundown, they brought to him all who were sick or possessed with demons. And the whole city was gathered together about the door. And he healed many who were sick with various diseases, and cast out many demons; and he would not permit the demons to speak, because they knew him" (Mark 1:32–34). The same pastoral attitude is likewise present in the apostles, who, by the power and mission conferred upon them by Christ, cured the sick and drove out demons (Mark 6:7).

The Gospels demonstrate a clear knowledge of the multiple spheres in which the action of Satan is developed. It is not by chance that they begin with the temptation of Christ in the desert, as they seek to make evident the dangerous activity of the evil one. The Gospel accounts point out the damage the devil causes in the spiritual realm when he steals the seed of the Word of God from souls (Matt. 13:19) or sows tares in the wheat field (Matt. 13:39). They describe the possession of the heart, as in the cases of Mary Magdalene (Mark 16:9), Judas (Luke 22:3), and Ananias (Acts 5:3). The evangelists show how Satan sows error through false prophets and so hampers the plans of God and persecutes the Church, as has been previously demonstrated. It is the great light of Christ that manifests to us the multiple and hidden activities of the evil one against man.

Here it is necessary to emphasize that the evangelists, in particular Luke, who was a physician, distinguish with precision the people affected by normal illnesses from those whose infirmities are caused by the demon. All the persons who suffer common illnesses have nothing to do with "the possessed" who experience a situation absolutely unique in its dramatic nature. Jesus, in this field that is practically inaccessible to human inquiry, demonstrates a capacity for diagnosing demonic possession which only His supernatural science could offer him.

Early in Matthew's Gospel, you find Jesus healing two blind men, touching their eyes and restoring their sight because of their faith (Matt. 9:27–31). Immediately after this, a mute is presented to Him. Jesus does not heal in the same manner as before because here the man was a "demoniac." Jesus first drives out the demon, and then the mute begins to speak (Matt. 9:32–33). This is still a sickness, but it does not have natural origins but rather preternatural ones. The Gospels teach with exactitude concerning this mysterious "spirit of infirmity" (Luke 13:11), whose existence today we tend to deny.

Diverse and many are the cases of the possessed. Without entering into a particularized analysis of them, it should be noted that some of them produce an intense drama, such as the possessed man at Gerasa (Mark 5:1–20) or the youth whom the disciples were unable to liberate (Luke 9:37–43). Even more striking is the intense activity of Jesus as an exorcist. Today, there is a tendency to claim that cases of possession are entirely exceptional. This claim, however, is in need of examination. Of course, the warning of the Church to ascertain whether it is the presence of the evil one or an illness (CCC 1673) must be taken seriously, but nothing impels one to conclude that the possessed are a rarity.

It makes a certain impression on the man of today to read in the Gospels that Jesus habitually drove out "many demons" from people who came to Him. The apostles engaged in the same activity, as in the case of Philip, who drove out many unclean spirits from many possessed (Acts 8:7). Jesus and His disciples' activity of exorcism is so intense that it comes to us on almost every page of the Gospels, and it is a sphere quite different from that of sickness. Were diabolic possessions more frequent then than now? There is no reason to think so. Nevertheless, the New Testament enumerates so many cases because the presence of God in Jesus Christ forced the demons to manifest themselves and to flee at the mere mention of His name. Now the situation of darkness and disbelief allows them to remain hidden in the hearts and members of people, tranquil in the certainty of being undisturbed.

The presence of the Son of God in this world is the beginning of the ruin of the kingdom of darkness. Jesus saw "Satan fall like lightning from heaven" (Luke 10:18). Now, until the definitive defeat of the forces of evil, the power of the King of kings and the Lord of lords is present on earth (Rev. 17:14). Thanks to the presence of the Son, the children of adoption can ask the Father that His Kingdom come; now they can invoke it, asking to be liberated from evil. It is Jesus Himself who invites us to pray with His words to the celestial Father so that the evil one can do nothing against us, with the certainty that our prayer will be heard.

"In this petition, evil is not an abstraction, but refers to a person, Satan, the Evil One, the angel who opposes God. The devil (*dia-bolos*) is the one who 'throws himself across' God's plan and his work of salvation accomplished in Christ" (CCC 2851). With the invocation "deliver us from evil," Jesus has put into our hands the weapon to defend ourselves against the multiple snares of the devil: from temptations, deceptions, aggressions, and various disturbances of soul and body. Invoking the Father with faith, we unite ourselves to the very prayer of Jesus for His disciples: "I do not pray that thou shouldst take them out of the world, but that thou shouldst keep them from the evil one" (John 17:15).

The Prayer of Liberation

It is necessary for the faithful to rediscover in all its value the prayer of liberation, which is included in the Our Father. The expressions "Thy Kingdom come . . . do not lead us into temptation, but deliver us from evil" must be seen in light of Christ's victory over Satan. These words make Christ's victory present in the lives of all those who pronounce them with faith. In the innumerable circumstances of life in which the evil one works, tempting, snaring, disturbing, oppressing, and causing damage to persons, things, and society, what better weapon than that simple yet efficacious prayer of Jesus Himself to liberate us from the evil one?

> Such a battle and such a victory become possible only through prayer. It is by his prayer that Jesus vanquishes the tempter, both at the outset of his public mission and in the ultimate struggle of his agony.... He urges us to vigilance of the heart in communion with his own. Vigilance is "custody of the heart," and Jesus prayed for us to the Father: "Keep them in your name." The Holy Spirit constantly seeks to awaken us to keep watch. Finally, this petition takes on all its dramatic meaning in relation to the last temptation of our earthly battle; it asks for final perseverance. "Lo, I am coming like a thief! Blessed is he who is awake. (CCC 2849).

Today, in a world in which faith and charity are disappearing, the demon works more than ever, and an uncountable multitude of persons must rediscover the weapons for the battle. Nothing is more important in the struggle against Satan than a prayer made with faith, regular reception of the sacraments, in particular Confession and Communion, and a morally elevated Christian life, in which the primary commitment is living in God's grace. When the Christian is strong, the demon is weak.

Of course, even a priest's blessing, which many faithful seek on occasions of particular disturbances (commonly attributed to spells, witchcraft, or curses), has its efficacy, as do the invocations of liberation made in groups or in families; but none of these can substitute for your prayer and your personal commitment as a Christian to bring you closer to Christ and allow His victory to work in your life. If the demonic disturbances continue, do not be discouraged, and do not make the mistake of making use of remedies worse than the evil you are suffering, as many do by going to occultists. The most important thing is that you progress in your faith. This is your victory, even though you have to carry the cross of the evil one's persecutions for a time.

Exorcism

In verified cases of diabolic possession, the Church provides a solemn and public prayer called exorcism. The priest exorcist orders Satan, in the name of God or of Christ, and through the authority given by the Church, to abandon the victim of the diabolic possession or obsession. The new Roman Ritual on exorcism, promulgated by Pope St. John Paul II, allows the use of modern language and launches anew this sacramental which had risked falling into disuse.

The *Catechism* explains:

> When the Church asks publicly and authoritatively in the name of Jesus Christ that a person or object be protected against the power of the Evil One and withdrawn from his dominion, it is called exorcism. Jesus performed exorcisms and from him the Church has received the power and office of exorcizing. In a simple form, exorcism is performed at the celebration of Baptism. The solemn exorcism, called "a major exorcism," can be performed only by a priest and with the permission of the bishop. The priest must proceed with prudence, strictly observing the rules established by the Church. Exorcism is directed at the expulsion of demons or to the liberation from demonic possession through the spiritual authority

> which Jesus entrusted to his Church. Illness, especially psychological illness, is a very different matter; treating this is the concern of medical science. Therefore, before an exorcism is performed, it is important to ascertain that one is dealing with the presence of the Evil One, and not an illness. (1673)

Solemn exorcism is opened with the aspersion of holy water, the symbol of baptismal purification. Some litanies follow, in which the blessing of God is implored and the victory of Jesus Christ over the evil one is celebrated. After the reading of the Gospel, the exorcist imposes his hands on the possessed person and invokes the power of the Holy Spirit so that the demon comes out of the person. Other prayers are recited, and the exorcist shows the crucifix to the possessed person and traces the sign of the cross on him to indicate the power of Christ over the devil. He then says the so-called deprecative formula, by which God is implored, followed by the "imperative" formula, by which Satan is directly ordered to leave the possessed. This is the culminating moment, in which the priest exorcist manifests the power of God, Christ, and the Church over the demons. After the liberation from diabolic possession has happened, the Magnificat or the Benedictus are sung.

Perhaps you are wondering how it is possible to ascertain whether we are witnessing a true diabolic possession or whether someone is suffering from a psychological sickness. The Church, in collaboration with scientific and psychiatric experts, has accumulated a solid experience of the signs that indicate a possible possession by the evil one, such as speaking unknown languages, revealing knowledge about things that are hidden or are far away, and demonstrating a physical strength that is superior in respect to the age or the health of the person. Further, the exorcist must consider the moral and spiritual state of the person being examined, such as, for example, a visceral aversion to God, Jesus Christ, the Virgin Mary, the saints, the Church, holy objects, and sacred images.

The devastating presence of Satan in persons and places is different and, therefore, much more serious than those disturbances of persons who believe themselves to be objects of spells, witchcraft, and curses worked by others. When a moral certainty of Satan's presence is ascertained, then, with the authority of the bishop, the priest can proceed to an exorcism, but with reserve and without publicity, in such a way that no one would consider this rite a form of magic or superstition.

The Prayer of Healing

The invocation "Deliver us from evil" includes not only the prayer of liberation from the evil one but also that of recovery from illness. Sickness is always a foreshadowing of death, which will come sooner or later, reminding us that "through the devil's envy death entered the world" (Wisd. 2:24). God desires that our hearts raise up an invocation for the healing of sicknesses, even though his Divine Wisdom disposes it for the greater good of our souls.

The invocations are extraordinary and brief, yet deep and efficacious, with which in Sacred Scripture God is asked for the body's healing. "Heal her, O God" (Num. 12:13), cried Moses, nearly ordering the Omnipotent to return health to his sister Miriam, who was struck with leprosy. "Heal me, O Lord, and I shall be healed" (Jer. 17:14), the prophet Jeremiah asked with confidence. "Lord my God, I cried to thee for help, and thou hast healed me" (Ps. 30:2), the psalmist exclaimed in acknowledgment.

The Lord voluntarily hears the invocations of whoever is suffering. "I am the LORD, your healer" (Exod. 15:26), God assures the people as they are going through the desert. It is a promise that runs through the entire history of salvation until its culmination in Jesus, who makes the healing of the sick a fundamental aspect of His ministry.

The healings worked by Jesus and the apostles are innumerable. The New Testament is completely interwoven with them, because physical healing and liberation from the demon are visible signs from God to men that salvation has come. They emerge in the simpler and more immediate world as convictions of God's power. The story of a leper's healing is enough for everyone: "While he was in one of the cities, there came a man full of leprosy; and when he saw Jesus, he fell on his face and besought him, 'Lord, if you will, you can make me clean.' And he stretched out his hand, and touched him, saying, 'I will; be clean.' And immediately the leprosy left him" (Luke 5:12–13). Dear friend, consider the faith and essence of the prayer and, at the same time, the merciful and immediate response of Jesus. The relationship of Jesus with the sick until the end of the world appears here in all its sober beauty.

Even though sin seems to be constantly increasing here on earth, and we know that the world is under the power of the evil one (1 John 5:19), the light of faith shows us the Victor, with whose strength even we can obtain the victory. Neither temptation, nor deception, nor persecution, nor any work of the evil one will ever be able to separate us from the love of Christ (see Rom. 8:38–39).

The *Catechism* tells us:

> When we ask to be delivered from the Evil One, we pray as well to be freed from all evils, present, past, and future,

of which he is the author or instigator. In this final petition, the Church brings before the Father all the distress of the world. Along with deliverance from the evils that overwhelm humanity, she implores the precious gift of peace and the grace of perseverance in expectation of Christ's return. By praying in this way, she anticipates in humility of faith the gathering together of everyone and everything in him who has "the keys of Death and Hades," who "is and who was and who is to come, the Almighty." (CCC 2854)

21

The Last Battle

The Hour of Death

Among all the hours of life, that of death is by far the most important. Indeed, in those dramatic moments, our eternal destiny is decided. It is not by chance that the last phases of a fatal illness are called an *agony*, which means "struggle." It is not just the natural struggle between the power of life and the forces of death but also and above all between the power of good and the power of evil. It will be the attitude we have before God at the instant of death that will determine the eternal fate of our soul.

According to the light of faith, death is not a natural phenomenon. God had given man the gift of immortality, which he has lost because of sin. "Through the devil's envy death entered the world" (Wisd. 2:24). Satan, enticing our first parents to sin, deprived them of all their divine gifts, particularly of sanctifying grace and of exemption from suffering, from sickness, and from death. In this way, the natural common experience of all living beings that grow old in time is death, which has become the "wages of sin" (Rom. 6:23). It is, therefore, "the last enemy" of man that must be defeated (1 Cor. 15:26).

Satan sees in the death of man the sign of his ancient victory and, at the same time, his last chance to grab our souls. Never as in that moment does he strive to keep those souls that he has captured by tempting man to evil. At the same time, he assaults the just with renewed fury, hoping to obtain at this extreme moment the victory that had eluded him before. Hell is mobilized around the death of a man, as the spiritual tradition tells us. Death has maintained all of its dramatic value, even during our superficial times, which makes death something banal and hides it from our eyes with a fig leaf.

However, death is also the great occasion of God and of His Divine Mercy. The obedience of Jesus has transformed the curse of death into a blessing (Mark 14:33–34). In their last instants, those who have let themselves be snared by satanic seduction see life in its reality. Of what use are riches, or the honors of the world, or the pleasures of the flesh, or any of the other things Satan offers to make us forget about God and eternal life? Man is alone and poor at the moment of death. He touches with his hand his dimension as a creature. The false myths that have fed his life are dissolved. He has no more future in front of him, save the one offered by eternity. How will it be? What will be waiting for me? All ask themselves this question at the supreme moment. The decisions that count can be postponed no longer, and it is at this moment that grace works its grandest miracles.

Nowadays, the principal concern is "helping" people to die without suffering and without their even noticing it. The dominant mentality seeks to make man die in the same way he is made to live, that is, without awareness. One lives by placing between parentheses and burying in the collective unconscious the problems pertaining to the sense of life. Consequently, one dies in the same way an animal comes to the end of its life, without grasping the decisive meaning of the event. Nevertheless, in spite of our "pitiful" lies, the dying person perceives in his heart the throbbing of the great battle that is being waged for his soul. Heaven and Hell face each other for the final duel. Our help could be definitive in determining the final destiny of our dear ones.

Today, many times we leave the dying alone in front of eternity, without upholding them in "the last temptation of our earthly battle" (CCC 2849). How much greater was solidarity when death was surrounded by the faith and the prayers of family and the religious comforts were the victorious weapons of the last battle! Death is the door to eternity. Whether it will be an eternity of blessing or one that is cursed will all depend on how the ultimate threshold is faced.

The Death of the Just and the Death of the Impious

There are two very different ways to die, just as there are two opposite ways to live. There is the death of the just, but there is also the death of the impious. There is the death of the one who dies in the Lord, which is filled with peace and hope, and there is death of one who has lived without God, which is opened up to an abyss of darkness and fear. In that instant, life comes to a conclusion, and all choices of the past push for the definitive decision. Whoever in life has decided for God will have no difficulty reaffirming this orientation at his last and decisive moment. Whoever, however, has behaved as if God did not exist can be saved only by a miracle of infinite Mercy.

Our generation has lost its perception regarding the seriousness and the immensity of this solemn moment. All deaths are equal in our eyes. No longer is it asked if a person has died in faith and prayer, but only if and how much he has suffered. Let us think about the immense suffering of Christ on the Cross, as well as the two thieves crucified with Him, one on His right and the other on His left. Yet the Gospel pays attention only to the motions of their hearts and the sentiments of their souls. Confronted by a scene like the one of the Crucifixion, which would offer the possibility of very sorrowful considerations of physical suffering, the Gospel reserves its attention to the spiritual drama with which life is concluded.

The death of Jesus is that of the just par excellence. Having passed through temptations, tests, and unimaginable sufferings, He dies completely entrusting Himself to the Father, whose will He has completely fulfilled here on earth. It there a more tragic death than that of Jesus? What death could be compared to His? All the darkness of the world weighed on His heart. Nevertheless, we see what divine peace emanates from His last words, with which He crosses the threshold of eternal light. "It was now about the sixth hour and there was darkness over the whole land until the ninth hour, while the sun's light failed; and the curtain of the temple was torn in two. Then Jesus, crying with a loud voice, said, 'Father, into thy hands I commit my spirit'" (Luke 23:44–46).

Here, there is redemption from the curse of death. Dying like Jesus, and with Jesus, death becomes the doorway to life. The evangelist Luke takes time to consider the last moments of the two thieves, so different from one another: "One of the criminals who were hanging railed at him, saying, 'Are you not the Christ? Save yourself and us!' But the other rebuked him, saying, 'Do you not fear God, since you are under the same sentence of condemnation? And we indeed justly; for we are receiving the due reward of our deeds; but this man has done nothing wrong.' And he said, 'Jesus, remember me when you come in your kingly power.' And he said to him, 'Truly, I say to you, today you will be with me in Paradise'" (Luke 23:39–43).

The first malefactor spent his life far away from God and dies closed off from His mercy. Was it not a rare grace to die next to the Redeemer of the world? But he even blasphemes him, dying in the darkness in which he had lived. The other, who also had a life of sin on his shoulders, opens his heart to the grace of faith and contrition and makes his death a transition into eternity. Both had the gift of being next to the Lord and Savior. If one is saved and the other lost, it is completely because of their personal decisions. In that extreme instant, grace knocks yet another time, even on the most hardened hearts. It is our answer which decides the eternal destiny of our souls.

The Final Temptation

If Satan is active and untiring along the entire arc of a person's life, he is particularly so in the time preceding death. He realizes that the final days of a man's life are a moment of great grace. God prepares people for their passage into eternity, even if they are unaware. The Divine Mercy watches over every soul and uses every small hole to open them up to the light of hope. Only those souls will be lost who, at the last instant, will have rejected the love of God, despairing of His forgiveness. The evil one makes recourse to all his infernal arts to impede the contrition of the sinner and to strike the just with the arrows of doubt and anguish.

The action of the demon is enormously facilitated by the state of spiritual abandonment and solitude in which the dying are left. A pagan mentality, which conditions even believers, entices one to look at the death of a person as the natural end of his life on earth. The only worries are for the body and all that relates to it. Few seem to think that in the instant of death itself, a person is judged by God and immediately sent to his eternal destiny (CCC 1022).

Even believers hesitate to prepare the dying at the decisive moment with prayer, acts of faith, and acts of abandonment to God. It is not considered that the dying person is approaching the most solemn instant of life, when he will be presented before the tribunal of Christ (2 Cor. 5:10). The time of pilgrimage has expired, and the spiritual state in which the soul is separated from the body will remain for all eternity. Before the instant of death, the greatest miracles of conversion are still possible. A brief invocation of pardon, a glance at the crucifix, or the grasping of a rosary between the hands are enough to offer to the Divine Mercy the necessary small opening to filter the light of God into the darkness with which the evil one surrounds the souls of sinners.

Satan attempts to create spiritual emptiness around the agonizing person, leaving him without the comfort of the sacraments (Confession, Communion, and the Anointing of the Sick) or the prayers of those who are around him. In this atmosphere, Satan can unravel his ominous action undisturbed, with the greatest danger for the soul left at the mercy of his frightening ferocity. This advantageous situation for him is turned upside down when someone is willing to assist the dying with love, suggesting to them the prayers of confidence in God, helping them to ask for His forgiveness, and offering prayers that would entrust them to the Divine Mercy. At times, a mere Ave Maria is enough to reawaken a glimmer of faith buried under the blanket of long neglect. When the heart has begun to open itself to prayer, it will be much easier, even for those further away, to dispose themselves to receive Confession and Communion.

Every one of us will arrive at this moment, and we will be better prepared to face it if we have known how to help people who are close to us and have accompanied them to the threshold of judgment. A proverb affirms that we die in the same way that we have lived. This is certainly valid for anyone who has traveled the right way in the course of his life. The beginning of eternity, seen in the light of faith, is not frightening because it is the meeting with the God we haved loved and served during our whole lives.

Nevertheless, the evil one seeks to lay snares even for the death of the just. He does it by insinuating doubts about the afterlife or evoking past sins already confessed and absolved, with the aim of oppressing and sowing doubts about forgiveness received. Even some saints have been attacked by Satan until the moment of their sweet meeting with the Lord. If during your life you have made acts of faith in the merciful Love and have asked for the grace of perseverance, along with the grace of perfect contrition, you will pass through the snares of the last temptation unscathed.

Arriving at the threshold of eternity unprepared represents a very serious danger. God has already passed by many times knocking on the door of your heart and waiting in vain for it to open. His immense goodness will drive Him to knock one more time. But will He find ears disposed to listen? It is an easy game for the evil one when a soul arrives at the supreme instant without faith, without hope, and without repentance. An act of humility, by which one recognizes himself as a sinner, would be enough to obtain salvation. The image of the good thief must be present in the mind of the person facing the final battle.

In fact, the sin by which a person is lost is that of distrusting the Merciful One. Any sin a man may have committed is forgiven him if he is repentant from the heart. Even Judas could have been absolved if he had asked for pardon, rather than hanging himself (Matt. 27:5). Satan's winning card is desperation. He will do everything to convince you that it is now too late and that there is no possibility of redemption. He will reclaim his ownership over you and his right to take you with him to his kingdom of perdition. But think about the criminal crucified to the right of Jesus and his humble request for salvation. Jesus will give Paradise even to you as He gave it to the good thief, because every sin has been redeemed and every life ransomed through the sufferings of Jesus Christ.

"Pray for Us Sinners"

It is very difficult to find a Catholic who has never recited an Ave Maria in the course of his life. In the second part of this celestial prayer, we ask the Mother of God to pray for us sinners "now and at the hour of our death." Even if we have prayed it distractedly, Mary, who by the will of God became our Mother, will take our prayers seriously and will be at our side in the decisive moment of the final temptation to protect us from the final assault of the evil one. Her presence, along with the presence of her most chaste spouse, St. Joseph, patron of a happy death, will be the safest guarantee of that victory which will lead us into eternal life (CCC 1014).

To protect us from the snares of the evil one, which accompany us throughout the course of our travailed existence, God has entrusted us to the maternal love of Mary. Whoever accepts her as mother and lets her guide him along the way of salvation without ever abandoning her can reasonably cultivate an intimate certainty of reaching the goal. Satan, who, with the collaboration of Eve, had dragged humanity into ruin, is now humiliated by the woman who is the faithful collaborator of Christ in the work of salvation.

Entrusting ourselves to the Virgin Mary, in such a way that she is a mother to us and we are her children, is the most efficacious weapon against Satan. The tempter is too shrewd for our poor capacities, and whoever has presumed to fight him without the simplicity, meekness, and purity of the Mother of God has sooner or later been tricked and overturned.

Mary most holy will teach us how to use the weapons of light to defeat the evil one. At her school, one learns everything necessary for discovering and defeating the tempter. Many who have presumed to venture on the way of sanctity without the help of the Virgin have been deceived and led astray, but Satan is not successful in deceiving and capturing the children of Mary.

You, most dear friend, stay under her mantle, where the darts of the enemy cannot reach you, and walk holding her hand. You will not miss the goal of life, the eternal salvation of the soul.

22

The End Times

"Be Ready"

God has not left us in the darkness regarding the future. The Sacred Scriptures contain prophecies, the majority of which come from the very mouth of Christ, that reveal to us the unfolding of future events. They shed a great light on the way of humanity, and the Christian finds in all of them whatever God has deemed useful to manifest to us for our salvation. Tomorrow is known only to God, and whatever He has chosen to communicate to us is already contained in His divine revelation.[8]

The first and fundamental truth of the Faith, with which the Bible comes to an end, concerns the conclusion of human history. The way of man on earth will end with the Second Coming of Christ. It will be a glorious, sudden, and conclusive event. "For the Son of man is to come with his angels in the glory of his Father, and then he will repay every man for what he has

[8] For an elaboration on the theme of the end of the world, see my book: *Dies Irae: I giorni dell'Anticristo* (Milan: Sugarco Edizioni, 1999). Published in English with the title *Wrath of God: The Days of the Antichrist* (Fort Collins, CO: Roman Catholic Books, 1998).

done" (Matt. 16:27). Human history will not end by the natural exhaustion of the cycle of life but by a supernatural occurrence, in which all men will be called before the tribunal of Christ for the Final Judgment (Matt. 25:31).

Another truth of the Faith, closely connected to the preceding one, concerns the time of this coming. God leaves us some signs so that we can reflect on that time, but we are unable to determine it with certainty. Jesus, in this regard, uses very precise language, which has been regrettably unsuccessful in discouraging continuous and recurring attempts to set the day of His coming. "He said to them, 'It is not for you to know times or seasons which the Father has fixed by his own authority" (Acts 1:7). The attitude of believers oscillates between the frantic curiosity of sectarian groups and the spiritual laziness of a sedentary Christianity. Thus, Jesus shakes us when He says: "Therefore, you also must be ready; for the Son of man is coming at an hour you do not expect" (Matt. 24:44).

In reality, the Second Coming of Christ is continuously impending on the way of men and on the future of the world. The conclusion of human history is in the hands of God, as is the life of every man. Just as at our personal death Christ calls us to Himself, in the same way with His Second Coming He convenes all of humanity for the Day of Judgment. Then the dead will rise, and it will be said to them, "come forth, those who have done good, to the resurrection of life, and those who have done evil, to the resurrection of judgment" (John 5:29).

Jesus has also revealed the characteristics of that time, from His first coming in the humility of the flesh to the last one in divine glory. It will be the time of grace and mercy: thus the Church, against which the gates of Hell will not prevail (Matt. 16:18), pours forth on men the light of revealed truth and the living water of love. It is the time in which men of every race, language, people, and nation will be welcomed by God and pardoned, reconciled, and clothed with the glory of divine grace.

Nevertheless, during this blessed and saving time of God, the "mystery of iniquity" (2 Thess. 2:7, Douay-Rheims), which tempts man to evil and causes him to pass through the crucible of seduction and of the test, can still act. Jesus prophesied on more than one occasion that His followers would be persecuted: "But before all this they will lay their hands on you and persecute you, delivering you up to the synagogues and prisons, and you will be brought before kings and governors for my name's sake" (Luke 21:12).

Christians are fundamentally optimistic, inasmuch as we understand this phase of history as a time of great grace. God has made His dwelling in the midst of us, assuming human nature and sharing the very core our life, now solidly guarded by His love. Nevertheless, we know that we must be vigilant, because the enemies (the world, the flesh, and the devil) are alive and operative, perfectly capable of dragging us down the road of perdition. Satan is unable to harm us, if we so wish, but his definitive defeat will be realized only at the end of time. And so at that moment, the evil one will unleash all his strength to seduce and destroy.

The Final Unleashing of the Forces of Evil

The New Testament not only reveals to us that the conclusion of human history will come together with the Second Coming of Christ in "power and great glory" (Matt. 24:30), but it also describes to us, in anticipation, the dramatic context of the occurrences immediately preceding the end of the world. Indeed, in the end times, the infernal powers will deliver the extreme and desperate attack against God and His work of salvation in the illusory attempt to hinder and destroy the plans of the Merciful One.

The satanic seduction will be manifested to the highest degree, with the objective of extinguishing the light of faith and the flame of charity. "And many false prophets will arise and lead many astray. And because wickedness is multiplied, most men's love will grow cold. But he who endures to the end will be saved" (Matt. 24:11–13). Exactly in this way, the unsurpassable deceiver will obtain his greatest results, and so Jesus has posed an unsettling question, left without a response: "Nevertheless, when the Son of man comes, will he find faith on earth?" (Luke 18:8).

The Scriptures insist on this final spectacular success of the great deceiver, even to the point of speaking of an almost total apostasy of humanity that rejects its Redeemer: "Men worshiped the dragon, for he had given his authority to the beast, and they worshiped the beast ... all who dwell on earth will worship it, every one whose name has not been written before the foundation of the world in the book of life of the Lamb that was slain" (Rev. 13:4, 8).

The end times will be the greatest test of faith for believers. Humanity will remain ensnared by the greatest satanic imposture: the illusion of men's ability to save themselves, with no need for God. "Before Christ's second coming the Church must pass through a final trial that will shake the faith of many believers. The persecution that accompanies her pilgrimage on earth will unveil the 'mystery of iniquity' in the form of a religious deception offering men an apparent solution to their problems at the price of apostasy from the truth. The supreme religious deception is that of the Antichrist, a pseudo-messianism by which man glorifies himself in place of God and of his Messiah come in the flesh" (CCC 675).

Nevertheless, at least a small flock of the faithful will remain firm in the truth, since the forces of Hell, by the explicit promise of Christ, will not be able to destroy the whole of the Church and extinguish the light of divine truth on earth. Satan will seek to destroy whomever he is unable to seduce, unleashing the most tremendous and destructive of persecutions: "The Church will enter the glory of the kingdom only through this final Passover, when she will follow her Lord in his death and Resurrection. The kingdom will be fulfilled, then, not by a historic triumph of the Church through a progressive ascendancy, but only by God's victory over the final unleashing of evil, which will cause his Bride to come down from heaven. God's triumph over the revolt of evil will take the form of the Last Judgment after the final cosmic upheaval of this passing world" (CCC 677).

The final times will be such that believers will have to invoke the grace of martyrdom. In fact, the Church, in its faithful remnant, is called to resist the fury of the evil one, who will throw himself against them with the same violence with which he attacked Christ, taking Him to the scaffold of the Cross. The Christians predestined to pass through "the great tribulation" consequently will be called to give that supreme testimony of faith and love as Jesus did, that is, until "the shedding of blood" (see Rev. 7:14; Heb. 9:22).

Perhaps Satan, blinded by his unmeasured and puffed up pride from having received the adoration of the people of earth, will think he has finally won, as he was deceived after seeing Christ nailed to the wood of the Cross. Even Christ's followers betrayed Him, save a meager little group, formed prevalently by women, who stayed not very far from the Cross. Now a similar scene is once again proposed, with the betrayal of many who have apostatized. They will follow "the man of lawlessness," "the son of perdition," whose coming "by the activity of Satan will be with all power and with pretended signs and wonders, and with all wicked deception" (2 Thess. 2:1–12).

But then when "the great dragon [who] was thrown down, that ancient serpent, who is called the Devil and Satan, the deceiver of the whole world" (Rev. 12:9) thinks that he has defeated God, "the Lord Jesus will slay him with the breath of his mouth and destroy him by his appearing and his coming" (2 Thess. 2:8).

The Definitive Defeat of Satan

When Christ comes in the glory of God, He will pronounce his solemn and definitive "It is enough!" against the powers of Hell. The first coming of Christ in the humanity of the flesh inaugurated the Kingdom of God without, however, impeding the enemy from sowing his discord. The demon can still exercise his work of seduction and perdition of souls, but he also can be defeated by the power of prayer and grace.

With the end of the world and the Last Judgment, the journey of humanity will be concluded. The just will enter into eternal life, while the impious will go with Satan to eternal torment (Matt. 25:46). The words of Christ concerning this are so explicit and peremptory that they cannot be contested: "Come, O blessed of my Father, inherit the kingdom prepared for you from the foundation of the world," says the Son of man, turning toward the good. Then turning toward the wicked, He pronounces words they will seek in vain to cancel from the Gospel: "Depart from me, you cursed, into the eternal fire prepared for the devil and his angels" (Matt. 25:34, 41).

In the Last Judgment, Satan will not be destroyed but relegated to his reign of death which was built after his original rebellion. Members of this kingdom, which is commonly called

Hell, are the rebellious angels and those men who have refused God in this life and have died impenitent. They go with the prince of evil whom they have chosen to follow and to serve. Satan desired to build his own kingdom in opposition to God, and it has been granted to him. The Almighty respects, albeit with infinite sadness, the free choice of those who have preferred the demon to Him. Whoever has chosen God in life will have God as recompense, but whoever has chosen Satan will have Satan as recompense.

After the Last Judgment, the seducer will never again be able to cause harm. His dark kingdom will remain as a black hole in God's creation, in testimony to the gift of freedom. God indeed has taken a "risk" in creating truly free creatures, capable of resisting even His infinite love. The existence of Hell is a demonstration of how much God has risked in calling to life beings made in His image and likeness, endowed with intelligence and free will. It was not possible even for the Creator to obtain the free reception of His creatures' love without their having the real possibility of rejecting him. When the rational being pronounces this decisive, radical, and irreversible "no," Hell is generated in his heart, and he becomes integrated in the kingdom of death.

Divine revelation concedes nothing to the false and superficial pietism of some who hypothesize either a general amnesty from which both the demons and the souls of the damned would benefit or even their future "conversion." The hatred of Satan and his followers against God is inextinguishable, like the flames of Hell. God Himself reveals to us what the freely chosen destiny of those who have rejected Him will be.

After the last frightening rebellion of Satan and his inhabitants on earth, "fire came down from heaven and consumed them, and the devil who had deceived them was thrown into the lake of fire and brimstone where the beast and the false prophet were, and they were tormented day and night for ever and ever . . . and if any one's name was not found written in the book of life, he was thrown into the lake of fire" (Rev. 20:9–10, 15). As the author of the book of Revelation explains immediately after, those who in this life have been vile, unbelieving, abject, homicidal, immoral, sorcerers, idolaters, and liars shall receive their lot, which is the burning lake of fire and sulfur (Rev. 21:8).

The Eternity of Hell

The eternity of Hell is a truth of the Faith based on the words of Christ, who speaks on more than one occasion of the "eternal fire." Such a peremptory expression is taken up by the authors of the New Testament and explicitly taught by the Church, who since the first centuries has condemned any doctrine which affirms that the torment of the demons and impious men will be only temporary.

It is stated that the eternity of Hell is repugnant to human reason; the sin of a creature who by its nature is finite and limited cannot be punished with an eternal penalty. But we have to understand that the final root of the eternity of Hell is the "irrevocable" choice against God by Satan and his followers. As the choice of the just for God is irrevocable, so is the choice of the wicked. The possibility of a decision which is "forever" is not at all repugnant to reason.

Satan is in no way a "poor devil" who would like to enter Paradise if God would concede it to him, but rather he is "the antigod," the one who strenuously opposes the Creator and desires to be the god of his kingdom of darkness and death. Satan wishes neither to submit nor to convert. We likewise imitate him when we swear an eternal hatred against somebody. The logic of iniquity is that of an inextinguishable rancor, which is also possible to experience here on earth. Evil is an unfathomable "mystery" of hatred; it is eternal, as is love.

Today, we find people who seek to make meaningless the words of Christ by claiming that Hell is empty. It is a slogan used by fools, some who wish to deceive others as well as themselves. Hell, even more than a location, is an existential condition of spiritual death in radical opposition to God. The demons are in this condition, as are all those who die in mortal sin. Hell is already anticipated in the heart of whoever separates himself from God during life by doing evil.

The words of Christ and the teachings of the Church concerning Hell must be taken very seriously, because the eternal salvation of our souls is at stake: "The teaching of the Church affirms the existence of hell and its eternity. Immediately after death the souls of those who die in a state of mortal sin descend into hell, where they suffer the punishments of hell, 'eternal fire.' The chief punishment of hell is eternal separation from God, in whom alone man can possess the life and happiness for which he was created and for which he longs" (CCC 1035).

Conclusion

At the end of this ample meditation on the mystery of evil, it is necessary to widen our gaze to the infinite beauty and dazzling splendor of the divine plan of Creation and Redemption. This magnificent project of elevating creatures to participation in the divine nature at the heart of Trinitarian love is being wonderfully realized in Christ Jesus through the Church. At the end of time, the entire universe will be transfigured, and God will be all in all.

The existence of Hell is much more than a possibility: it is a reality for the demons and for men who die in conscious refusal of the merciful love of God. Nevertheless, even though it is a sorrowful reality, primarily for God, it is not enough to darken the work of the Creator's infinite love. The book of Revelation does not tell us how many are those who will be thrown with Satan into the lake of fire and sulfur, but it does tell us of the vast number of the elect in Heaven with unforgettable words: "After this I looked, and behold, a great multitude which no man could number, from every nation, from all tribes and peoples and tongues, standing before the throne and before the Lamb, clothed in white robes, with palm branches in their hands" (Rev. 7:9).

The gift of freedom has its price. God loves every man and offers to each one of us the grace of salvation. Freedom is a risk God has desired to take, but which renders life serious and worthy of being lived. Hell is not a failure of the divine work of Creation and Redemption but a testimony of God's courage in giving life to free creatures. How many persons will be saved or lost does not depend on God alone but also on us, who are called to be His collaborators.

The words of Christ on eternal perdition must be heard in their terrible seriousness, but, at the same time, they must serve to stimulate us to sacrifice our lives in total dedication as we cooperate in the eternal salvation of souls.

Sophia Institute

Sophia Institute is a nonprofit institution that seeks to nurture the spiritual, moral, and cultural life of souls and to spread the gospel of Christ in conformity with the authentic teachings of the Roman Catholic Church.

Sophia Institute Press fulfills this mission by offering translations, reprints, and new publications that afford readers a rich source of the enduring wisdom of mankind.

Sophia Institute also operates the popular online resource CatholicExchange.com. *Catholic Exchange* provides world news from a Catholic perspective as well as daily devotionals and articles that will help readers to grow in holiness and live a life consistent with the teachings of the Church.

In 2013, Sophia Institute launched Sophia Institute for Teachers to renew and rebuild Catholic culture through service to Catholic education. With the goal of nurturing the spiritual, moral, and cultural life of souls, and an abiding respect for the role and work of teachers, we strive to provide materials and programs that are at once enlightening to the mind and ennobling to the heart; faithful and complete, as well as useful and practical.

Sophia Institute gratefully recognizes the Solidarity Association for preserving and encouraging the growth of our apostolate over the course of many years. Without their generous and timely support, this book would not be in your hands.

www.SophiaInstitute.com
www.CatholicExchange.com
www.SophiaInstituteforTeachers.org

Sophia Institute Press® is a registered trademark of Sophia Institute.
Sophia Institute is a tax-exempt institution as defined by the Internal Revenue Code, Section 501(c)(3). Tax ID 22-2548708.